THE THIRD REICH

AND

THE CHRISTIAN CHURCHES

Edited by
PETER MATHESON

WILLIAM B. EERDMANS PUBLISHING COMPANY
Grand Rapids, Michigan

Library of Congress Cataloging in Publication Data

Main entry under title:

The Third Reich and the Christian churches.

Collection of documents translated from German.
1. Germany—Church history—1933-1945—Sources.
2. Church and state in Germany—1933-1945—Sources.
I. Matheson, Peter.
BR856.T44   274.3'823   80-26767
ISBN 0-8028-1872-2

THE THIRD REICH
AND
THE CHRISTIAN CHURCHES

Contents

Preface

The English-speaking world has been fortunate in its secondary works on the "Church Struggle" during the Third Reich, but source material has been far harder to come by. The aim of this collection is to provide those with no access to the massive German documentation already in print with a first reader on the subject. Explanatory notes have been kept brief.

Selection has not been easy. It is to be hoped that the balance is approximately right, chronologically, confessionally, and in other respects. Availability of other English translations has not been assumed.

Peter Matheson.

1 Programme of the NSDAP, 1920

Declared unalterable by Hitler in 1926, the Party Programme of 1920 became in fact of steadily diminishing value as an index of the real intentions of the NSDAP. Article 24, however, with its vague reference to 'positive Christianity', proved an invaluable tactical aid in convincing the Catholic and Protestant masses that they could support National Socialism without betraying their religious convictions.

Article 24:
We insist upon freedom for all religious confessions in the state, providing they do not endanger its existence or offend the German race's sense of decency and morality. The Party as such stands for a positive Christianity, without binding itself denominationally to a particular confession. It fights against the Jewish-materialistic spirit at home and abroad and believes that any lasting recovery of our people must be based on the spiritual principle: the welfare of the community comes before that of the individual.

Hermann Sasse, editor of the *Church Year Book* of 1932 commented on this article as follows:
". . . One can perhaps forgive National Socialism all its theological sins, but this article 24 excludes any possibility of a dialogue with the church, whether Protestant or Catholic. Rosenberg's *Myth of the 20th Century*, for all its blasphemies and its extravagant nonsense about the history of religions and of the world, is a harmless and venial lapse compared with this article; the same can be said of the whole theology of the swastika and the messianic cult of the Führer. Evangelical theology can enter into dialogue with the National Socialists on all the points of the Party programme, even about the Jewish question and its understanding of race, it may perhaps be able to take seriously the whole of the rest of the programme. About this article, however, no discussion at all is possible. . . . For the Protestant church would have to begin such a discussion with a frank admission that its doctrine constitutes a deliberate, permanent in-

1

sult to the 'German race's sense of decency and morality', and hence that she can have no expectation of tolerance in the Third Reich. . . ."

According to the Protestant doctrine of original sin, "the new-born infant of the noblest Germanic descent, endowed in body and mind with the optimal racial characteristics, is as much subject to eternal damnation as the genetically gravely compromised half-caste from two decadent races. And we must go on to confess that the doctrine of the justification of the sinner *sola gratia, sola fide,* is the end of Germanic morality just as it is the end of all human morality. . . . We are not much interested in whether the Party gives its support to Christianity, but we would like to know whether the church is to be permitted to preach the Gospel in the Third Reich without let or hindrance, whether, that is, we will be able to continue undisturbed with our insults to the Germanic or Germanistic moral sense, as with God's help we intend to do . . ."

2 Quousque Tandem? 1930

Karl Barth, Professor of Systematic Theology in Bonn, had become by 1930, when this article appeared, the leading spokesman of a small but articulate group within the Protestant Churches which challenged the traditional ethos of 'National Protestantism', by an abrasive call to return to the prophetic witness of the Biblical revelation. It was, above all, the ecclesiastical triumphalism of the Protestant establishment which provoked him to write this piece of fierce and gifted polemic.

Some weeks ago the following passage kept cropping up in our church newspapers and congregational newsletters. . . . Apparently it comes from the opening sentences of an article on the present situation of the church by Professor Schneider in the most recent volume of his *Church Year Book*:

"As Präses Dr. Wolff quite rightly says. . . . 'The evangelical church had dealt energetically with the monstrous threat to its very existence.' Indeed there was a time when — at least as far as its outward forms were concerned — it was literally faced with destruction, a time in which atheism was dutifully, if prema-

2

turely, preparing to hold a funeral oration over it. Some cock-sure gossipers from among the 'intellectuals' were not backward in suggesting the wording. The 'ordinary man' was remarkably silent at first, almost paralysed, unable to grasp at once what was going on before his eyes. But after a while it became clear that there were still 'church people', after all. . . . One thing became evident then — and has remained evident ever since: that an understanding for religion was in fact more profoundly rooted in the soul of the German people than outward appearances tended to suggest. The 'divine nevertheless' (*das heilige Dennoch*) has triumphed. What we call the empirical church has demonstrated both its flexibility and its powers of endurance. The conduct of church affairs in the last decade was a virtuoso performance. . . . We are far from being 'over the top' yet, but we have left behind us the narrow defile and can see open territory ahead."

Laying aside all professional long-windedness, discretion, and prudence, I have this comment to make:

It is a scandal which cries to heaven that the German evangelical church is always talking in this way. . . . Professor Schneider speaks for dozens of our church leaders and for hundreds and thousands of our pastors. I have nothing against him and those like him, but I have everything against the sort of language with which he and the army of those like him are leading this country astray. I am sick, too, of holding my peace. It is quite patent that such people have neither the time, the interest, nor the receptivity to listen to an indirect theological critique, for there has been no lack of this in the past ten years, and yet at the end of them they boast of their 'virtuoso performance', trumpeting forth without the least inhibition the triumph of the 'divine nevertheless'. . .

And so I will be crude and declare that language like this bears the mark of Catiline, of the really dangerous conspiracy against the very substance of the evangelical church. . . . If we allow ourselves to be constantly addressed in this way, if we fail to protest, if this language is listened to and given credence, then in its inmost being the Church has already ceased to live. . .

The evangelical church is already surrounded by a dark cloud of mistrust. Anyone who is not blind sees this. But its leaders are blind and do not see it. They rejoice in the confidence that a tiny group of 'church people' seems to put in them, coming to sit at their feet again and again on Sundays and feast days, full of expectancy. What they fail to see is that even, indeed above all, in the case of this good petit-bourgeois 'church people' only a remnant of trust is still there. This, too, can and will evaporate

3

should the irrelevance of all their churchmanship become evident . . .

Why is this sort of 'leadership' intolerable? Because its words and deeds show quite unambiguously that it is seeking its own ends, building itself up, blowing its own trumpet. The only way it differs from those clustered around other flags and pennants is the fact that — bloated by the claim to represent the cause of God — it can do so with much less interruption, with far fewer inhibitions, and much more blatantly. If it were concerned with the cause of God would it be able — with the complacency of someone reflecting on a recent bout of 'flu — to speak of the time — now fortunately over and done with — when 'it was literally faced with destruction'? Or to speak with such self-satisfied scorn (as if the great decline were only the fault of others) of those atheists, intellectuals and gossipers who made such a complete miscalculation earlier on? Or to speak with such broad complacency (as if it were not a miserable cliché) of the 'understanding of religion' so deeply rooted in the soul of the German people? Or with this near-blasphemous certainty about the 'divine nevertheless'? . . . Or with such hard-heartedness (as if there were no housing shortage and no unemployment in Germany) that she, she the church, is now 'out of the narrow defile' . . .

And meanwhile — you can be sure of this — what the Church should and could apply itself to, the preaching of the Gospel, will be neglected by comparison . . .; a church like this cannot be believed in a single word of her Christmas and Easter and Sunday preaching. When she says 'Jesus Christ', even if she says it a thousand times, all that will be heard is her own satiety and security, and she should not be surprised if with all her 'Jesus Christ' she is talking into the wind, blind to the real distress of real men, just as she is deaf to the Word of God, having made from all the exhortation, comfort, and teaching of the Bible and the Reformers water for her own little mills. . . . It is high time to stop taking this path, high time to retrace our steps. Quousque tandem?

3 Guiding Principles of the 'German Christians', 26 May 1932

The 'Faith Movement of German Christians', an amalgam of three small right-wing Protestant groupings, was

4

founded at the behest of the NSDAP to mobilise Protestants behind National Socialism and specifically to increase the influence of the Party in the Prussian Church elections of 1932. This first manifesto, of 26 May 1932, betrays its overwhelmingly political motivation.

1. The aim of these guiding principles is to indicate to all believing German men how and why the church should be restructured. These guiding principles are not intended to be or to replace a confession of faith, or to challenge the confessional basis of the Protestant church. They are a confession of life.
2. We campaign for a unification of the 29 churches gathered together under the 'German Protestant Church Federation' into one Protestant Reich Church . . .
3. Those campaigning as 'German Christians' have no intention of being the sort of political grouping usually found within the church up to now. They appeal to all Protestant Christians of German descent. The parliamentary era is out of date, in the church as well. . . . We want a dynamic national church (Volkskirche), which expresses the living faith of our people.
4. We stand on the basis of positive Christianity. Ours is an affirmative, truly national faith in Christ, in the Germanic spirit of Luther and of heroic piety.
5. We want to make the recovery of the German sense for life a reality in our church and to give our church real vitality. In the fateful struggle for the freedom and the future of Germany the leadership of the church has proved to be too weak. Up to now the church has not called men to the decisive battle against Marxism, the enemy of God, and against the unspiritual Centre group, but has concluded a church treaty with the political parties which represent these groupings. We want our church to be fighting in the forefront of the decisive battle for the existence or eclipse of our people. It must not stand aside, or even distance itself from the fighters for freedom.
7. In race, nation, and cultural heritage we see the orders of existence which God has given us in trust; it is the law of God that we should be concerned to preserve them. Therefore racial admixture is to be opposed . . . faith in Christ does not destroy the race, it deepens and sanctifies it.
8. Properly understood Home Mission is living, active Christianity. In our view, however, this is rooted not in mere

5

pity, but in obedience to God's will, and thanksgiving for Christ's death on the Cross. Mere pity is 'charity', which becomes a mixture of arrogance and of a bad conscience, and makes a nation soft. We are not unacquainted with Christian love and the obligation to the helpless, but we demand that the nation be protected from the feckless and the inferior. On no account must Home Mission contribute to the degeneration of our nation. . . .

9. We regard the mission to the Jews as a grave danger to our culture. Through its doors alien blood is imported into the body of our nation. It has no right to exist except as Overseas Mission. We oppose any mission to the Jews in Germany as long as the Jews have the right to citizenship and there is therefore a danger of bastardisation and an obscuring of racial differences. Holy Scripture also has something to say about righteous anger and the failure of love. In particular marriage between Germans and Jews must be prohibited.

10. We want a Protestant church rooted in our own culture, and are opposed to the spirit of a Christian cosmopolitanism. We want to overcome the degenerate phenomena which derive from this spirit — pacifism, international freemasonry, etc. — by faith in our nation's God-given mission. No Protestant clergyman may belong to a Masonic lodge . . .

4 The Roman Catholic Church and National Socialism, 17-19 August 1932

Unlike the Protestant Churches, the Catholic Church committed itself to a policy of official opposition to the National Socialist Party. This was partly due to its awareness that the Party's teachings and activities were incompatible with Catholicism, partly to the fact that, in the Centre Party, the Catholic Church already possessed a political arm. This explanation of its views was made by the meeting of all the German bishops at Fulda, 17-19 August 1932.

1. GENERAL PRINCIPLES

All the bishoprics have forbidden membership of this Party because:

(a) Parts of its official programme contain false teachings . . .
(b) Hostility to the Faith is evident in statements by countless leading figures and publicists of the Party, in particular a hostile attitude to fundamental doctrines and claims of the Catholic Church. These statements have never been refuted or criticised by the supreme leadership of the Party. The same is true of the attitude to the confessional school, Christian marriage, and similar questions.
(c) It is the unanimous conclusion of the Catholic clergy and of those genuinely concerned to further the interests of the Church in the public sphere that if the Party were to gain the monopoly of power in Germany which it is so hotly pursuing the prospects for the church interests of the Catholics would be gloomy indeed.
(d) Considerable numbers of people join the Party solely because of their support for the Party in the secular sphere, for its economic policies and political aims. But this cannot be justified. Support for the Party necessarily involves, whether one wants this or not, furthering its aims as a whole. Moreover the promises made by the Party appear to be incapable of fulfilment.

2. ATTITUDE TO PARTICULAR CASES

The individual pastor must exercise his discretion as to whether, in a particular case, paid-up membership of the Party can be excused, providing it does not involve any specific promotion of its cultural aims or any participation in its propaganda. It may, for example, be excusable as an erroneous view adopted in all innocence, or under the influence of a sort of mass psychosis, because of terrorist intimidation, or because a refusal might have fateful consequences . . .

5 The Altona Confession, 11 January 1933

When National Socialism emerged in 1930 as a serious political force it tended to be its populist radicalism, its 'socialism' rather than its nationalism which alienated the Protestant churches. After 1933 such opposition as Protestantism offered was generally of a conservative kind: a defence of traditional values and institutions. **This statement by a group of pastors in Altona, near Hamburg, shows, however, how genuinely theological concerns were bound to have political consequences in the Third Reich.**

Article 1: The Church

. . . the church cannot allow its inner being to be determined or influenced by the state or by a political party, by scholarship or by a *weltanschauung* of any kind. It must let the Word run free . . .

Anyone who expects the pastor to justify or support a particular type of economic organisation in his preaching, to advocate war or peace, the bearing of arms or the conscientious objection to military service — anyone who expects the pastor to declare without qualification that the loftiest deed of which a man is capable — a heroic death for his fatherland — is a blessed death, tempts him to deny the Lord Jesus Christ and His work of redemption. . .

Article 2: Man's Limitations

. . . we reject emphatically the dream of a coming earthly realm of justice, peace and general well-being in whatever form . . . . Whether it is the belief in the coming of an earthly realm of peace and security for all peoples, or in a classless society free of hunger, drudgery, and suffering, or in a future national state of complete justice and racial integrity — in each case the limits set by God are denied, political activity is distorted, and redemption in Christ esteemed lightly. . .

Article 3: The State

. . . Subjects have no cause for rejoicing if the government is weak. It will be to their disadvantage to live in an anarchic situation; they should do everything to increase the government's power and respect. We reject the view that the basis of the state is a 'social contract'. Any one who speaks thus does not realise that God has set the state above us.

We reject any divinisation of the state. If state authority lords itself over the conscience, it becomes anti-Christian . . .

Article 5: The Ordinances of God

. . . We believe it to be a divine ordinance that all ranks in society are bound together for better or for worse. Hence we regard it as sinful to regard employers and employees, state and civil servant, as objects of exploitation . . .

6 Policy Statement by Hitler, 23 March 1933

At first, Hitler lacked any precise policy in regard to the churches. He had, after all, more pressing business on his hands: unemployment, internal 'pacification', foreign policy. On the other hand he could not afford to neglect the vast reservoir of support which the churches could tap, and may well have hoped to remodel them to suit his purposes. The paragraphs about the churches in his broadcast were designed, therefore, to underline the 'responsible' nature of his régime and assure him of the loyal support of the churches until the other political parties were neutralised and totalitarianism firmly established.

The national government regards the two Christian confessions as the most important factors for the preservation of our national culture. It will honour the treaties concluded between them and the provincial governments. Their rights will not be infringed. It does, however, hope and trust that the work for the national and moral renewal of our nation, which the government has taken upon it, will for its part be given like approval. Its attitude to all the other confessions will be that of objective justice.

The national government will guarantee the Christian confessions their due influence in school and educational matters. It is concerned to foster a frank and harmonious relationship between church and state. The fight against a materialistic view of the world and for the creation of a genuine national community is as much in the interests of the German nation as of those of our Christian faith.

Likewise the government of the Reich, which regards Christianity as the unshakeable foundation of our national life and morality, regards the fostering and the extension of the friendly relations to the Holy See as a matter of the greatest importance.

The rights of the churches will not be restricted, nor will their relationship to the state be changed.

7 Cardinal Bertram to the German Archbishops, 1 April 1933

One of the first fruits of Hitler's conciliatory broadcast of

23 March 1933 came only five days later, when the Roman Catholic bishops dramatically reversed their previous policy of outright opposition to National Socialist politics. This decision to come to terms with the new political realities meant, in fact, the abandonment of the Centre Party. It was made less bitter by the hierarchy's distrust of the liberal and pluralistic spirit of the Weimar era, by a hankering after an authoritarian Christian state, and by a fervid anti-Communism.

Over the past few years the supreme shepherds of the German dioceses, in their proper concern to maintain the purity of the Catholic faith and preserve the vital interests and rights of the Catholic church, have with good cause adopted a disapproving attitude to the national Socialist movement, and have repeatedly explained why they have acted in this way. Their prohibitions and admonitions were intended to remain valid as long as the grounds for them still existed.

It has now to be recognised that in solemn, public pronouncements by the supreme representative of the Reich government, who at the same time is the authoritarian Leader of that movement, account was taken of the inviolability of Catholic doctrine and of the immutable obligations and rights of the church. Moreover the Reich government expressly recognised the complete validity of the concordats made between the church and the individual German provinces. Without therefore departing from the condemnation of certain religious and moral errors voiced in our earlier measures, the episcopate believes it has ground for confidence that the general prohibitions and admonitions mentioned above need no longer be regarded as necessary.

Catholic Christians, for whom the voice of their church is holy, have no need, even at the present time, for any special exhortation to be loyal to the legal authorities, to carry out their civic duties conscientiously, or to reject as a matter of principle all illegal or subversive activities.

The solemn pronouncements so often made to all Catholics, exhorting them to continual, vigilant, and sacrificial commitment to the peace and social welfare of the nation, to the upholding of Christian religion and morality, the freedom and rights of the Catholic church, and the maintenance of the confessional schools and Catholic youth organisations, remain as valid as ever . . .

10

8 Cardinal Bertram on the Boycott of Jewish Businesses, 1 April 1933

Lichtenberg was to be a consistent intercessor on behalf of the Jews, finally dying on his way to Dachau in 1943. More typical of the churches, however, is Bertram's concern that support for the Jews might compromise the church.

With a recommendation from Monsignor Lichtenberg, Dean of Berlin Cathedral, Herr Oscar Wassermann, the Director of the German Bank in Berlin (acting also in his capacity as President of the Inter-Confessional Working Party for Peace) called upon me today. He requested the intercession of the episcopate with the Reich President and the Reich government for the lifting of the boycott against all Jewish businesses. . . . On my remark that as an individual I have no remit from the episcopate to take any such step, and that I was not competent to assess the reasons given for the boycott, still less to make any prognosis as to its likely success or lack of success, he agreed that I should circulate at least their eminences the archbishops of the church provinces as to the advisability of such a step.

My hesitation rests on:

(a) the fact that this is a matter of economics, of measures directed against an interest group which has no very close bond with the church;

(b) the fact that such a step appears to be an intervention in an area which has little to do with the episcopate's field of activity; there are good grounds for the episcopate restricting itself to its own working area;

(c) the fact that the step is likely to be unsuccessful since the arguments *pro et contra* are already well enough known to the relevant authorities without any representations on our part;

(d) furthermore, there is the tactical consideration that this step, knowledge of which cannot be restricted to a small number of people, would certainly be given a highly invidious interpretation throughout Germany and in the most diverse quarters. In view of the extremely difficult and gloomy prospect generally, this certainly cannot be a matter of indifference.

One might mention in passing that the Press, which is overwhelmingly in Jewish hands, has remained consistently silent about the persecution of Catholics in various countries . . .

9 Appointment of Ludwig Müller by Hitler, 25 April 1933

Müller, a German Christian, was an altogether unknown figure when Hitler appointed him to be his special adviser on Protestant church affairs. He encouraged Hitler to think that it would be relatively easy to make the churches amenable to the Party's wishes, winning over the laity by the enthusiastic propaganda of the German Christians and thus isolating any obdurate or reactionary elements among the clergy.

Recent events have made it necessary to determine policy on a number of questions involving the relation of the state to the evangelical churches. In view of this I nominate as my representative for the affairs of the evangelical churches, in so far as they touch on these questions, the chaplain to the Königsberg military region, Herr Müller. He also has a particular responsibility for furthering all endeavours to create an Evangelical German Reich Church.

10 Central Office of the Federation of Protestant Churches, June 1933

The following memorandum, dated 7 June 1933, was circulated widely overseas by the central office of the Federation of Protestant Churches in Germany, although it did not gain the approval of the President, Dr. Kapler. It can be taken as reasonably representative of the anti-semitic sympathies within both of the major Christian confessions. Seldom, however, did the Churches allow themselves to be used so blatantly for the purposes of National Socialist propaganda as in this instance.

Memorandum on the Present Situation in Germany, with special reference to the Jewish Question

Over the last few months a revolution has taken place in Germany, which is still under way, or — to put it better — a rebirth of the nation with the most profound and far-reaching internal consequences. . . . As is the case with every political upheaval, the German revolution of 1933 is engendering new thinking about how the well-being and even the survival of the nation should be safeguarded. Hence a reappraisal of many aspects of cultural life is under way, frequently building on the basis of a prior but unpublicised change in attitudes. The deeper the intellectual roots of the revolution, the more radical this reappraisal has been . . .

The combination of liberal and Marxist ideas which set its stamp on the Constitution of post-war Germany did not prove fruitful for political or national life. Above all, it failed to resolve the dangerous social and political tensions which had for so long beset the German people. This disastrous situation is both the ultimate cause for the rise of the National Socialist movement and the supreme challenge which it faces. Here is the key to an understanding of what is now happening in Germany . . .

The German people has been fighting for its existence now for almost two decades. The aim of the government is to build up once more a vigorous, healthy organism, in place of the decrepit structures of our national life. This will require tremendous organisational and mental effort. Discipline and order, thrift and industry, social harmony and the nurture of the cultural resources native to the German people are both the means to and the end of this programme . . .

. . . .

As expected the government has recognised that one of its *chief internal tasks* is the intellectual and political defeat of Marxism, especially in the form of Communism, which had attained a degree of strength in Germany — and, incidentally, in other countries as well — thus consistuting an immediate threat to the state and to the churches, In the process, of course, the state has had to act with occasional harshness . . .

On the whole, however, it will be the verdict of history that, considering the vast changes which we have been experiencing, the course of events was a disciplined one. As was to be expected, however, in view of the momentum of the revolution and the depth of feeling among the population, certain acts of violence have taken place — against Jews, too, but not only or pre-eminently against them — which have been disapproved and regretted not only by the churches, but by the government as well. Yet they are nothing at all in comparison with the ghastly and shameful events of the 1918 revolution, which in contrast attracted not the least attention from the Christian world when they occurred . . .

13

In contrast to the 1918 revolution our national leaders now explicitly confess their loyalty to Christianity and Church . . .

If it is always difficult to visualise the situation of another country from the outside, especially in such a troubled time as ours, it is particularly true in relation to the *Jewish Question* that the real state of affairs can only be understood from within Germany, by those who have suffered together under the previous dispensation . . .

The Jewish problem in Germany is not really a post-war problem, although it was not until after the War, influenced on the one hand by the German revolution of 1918 and on the other by the Versailles Treaty, that it became as acute as it is today. A broad cross-section of the nation considered that the way in which various Jewish circles regarded the life and death struggle of our nation during the War was ambiguous or even hostile. On top of this came the fact that after the coup d'état of 1918 the Jews, thanks to their good relations with the Marxist parties, gained for themselves a disproportionately high number of public offices and other important positions in public life. . . . Then there was the further fact that the governments after 1918 threw open the Eastern frontiers to Jewish immigration and countless culturally inferior Jews from the East were able to settle in Germany or even secure German citizenship. Hand in hand with this went the Jewish infiltration of scholarship, journalism and literature, of theatre and film, while in many cases German scholars and artists were pushed into the background.

. . . .

But it was not only the disproportion between the total number of Jews and the number of important positions which they held which aroused such deep feeling in the nation; people began to realise that the Jewish mentality, so evident in literature, theatre and films, was undermining the Christian faith and ethic, family life and the national culture, indeed all those primal bonds without which it is impossible to ensure the survival of nation and state. One cannot stress too much the threat to Christian culture in particular which was mounted under the pretext of intellectual freedom . . .

Not only did all this help latent anti-semitic attitudes within the populace to gain the upper hand, it also forced those who thought more soberly to see that something must be done to protect our national heritage against this ever increasing danger. Jewish circles, incidentally, are also aware that some solution to this must be found. . . . One should not, however, look only at the negative aspects; there should, rather, be a recognition that anti-semitism is only the reverse side to much deep reflection about what is truly German and of a determination to structure the German state and destiny in a manner appropriate to this specifically German character . . .

News about isolated acts of violence against Jews in Germany has occasioned a propaganda campaign abroad, making use of fictitious and misleading material (and urging a boycott of German products) . . .

Since it was proved that the propaganda, which might well have had the dangerous consequence of destroying the whole fabric of international relations if it had continued much longer, had originated with or been energetically promoted by Jewish circles overseas, the leadership of the NSDAP decided to conduct a boycott of Jewish businessmen in Germany as a counter-measure.

. . . .

The law now promulgated contains stipulations which require the compulsory retiral of officials not of Aryan descent. . . . Whether any mitigation of this law can be expected, either soon or at a later point in time, cannot be said at the moment. It should, however, be realised that the hardships which some individuals will undergo as a result of these stipulations must be seen in the context of the widespread grave unemployment now rampant in Germany and particularly serious among those with academic qualifications, who are frequently destitute of both possessions and prospects . . .

One must conclude, then, that there is no question at the moment of any "persecution of the Jews" in Germany threatening their economic or personal survival. . . . The main feature of the measures taken is the defensive aim of safeguarding the German people. *There is no attack of any kind on the Jewish religion or on the free exercise of the Jewish cult* . . .

. . . .

It is self evident that the German Protestant Churches, confessing their allegiance to God's Word, condemn with all sharpness any act of violence or any insult directed against a fellow-countryman of another race . . .

It is, however, scarcely possible for any general comment to be made by the church about the state's treatment of the Jewish question in view of the complexity of the factors involved. It is, after all, doubtful whether and to what degree the church has any remit at all to make any general judgement about the question, especially since the legislative position is such as has been outlined above. From the point of view of the church there can be no simplistic approach to the unusual conditions in Germany, although this often seems to be assumed abroad. It is the primary responsibility of the state to decide what conditions it considers must be fulfilled before anyone can be entrusted with offices in the civil service or in other areas of importance for the national life. Especially, too, at a time like this, when the nation and the fatherland are in the process of being wrenched back by a strong hand from falling into the abyss, and when the prime and urgent need is to forge together into a common sense of national purpose the various parties, groups and classes which have hitherto been devoting their energies to tearing one another apart, it is the duty of the church to be particularly conscious in all its pronouncements on public matters of the incredible size of the task, and of the extraordinary difficulties and responsibilities with which the leadership of the state is burdened. The Gospel may well constrain the church to adopt just such an attitude . . .

Above all, the church will have to alleviate the lot of those Jewish Christians among its members who are in need by extending brotherly love to them. Much has already been done here — quietly, on the whole, and without publicity.

It should also be stressed that the legal position of the Jewish Christians in the German Protestant Provincial Churches has not been affected by the state legislation.

Church and theology have failed in the last few decades to deal with the Jewish question in sufficient seriousness and depth. What has been said on the matter from church quarters both at home and abroad seems to have been determined largely by *humanitarian* considerations, rather than evidencing any relationship to the Word of God. The church stands in the same danger here as it does when confronted by such phenomena as Communism and collectivism. In regard to them, too, the church is only equal to its task as church, when it draws the strength and justification for its stance from the depths of the *Gospel*. If there is, then, to be in the future a changed approach to the Jewish problem, this can only happen if all the churches really see the problem, and deal with it, in a theological manner, in the light of the Word of God.

11 **Easter Message of the Old Prussian Union, 16 April 1933**

The naive hopes and the distressingly vague language of this statement by the Executive Council of by far the largest of the twenty-eight Protestant provincial churches illustrates how they were swept along by the enthusiasm for the new régime. The reference to a revival of religion is reminiscent of the chauvinistic sermons of the First World War.

We know that all our comrades in the Protestant faith will rejoice with us that the breakthrough of the most profound energies of our people is finding expression in patriotic awareness, true national community, and religious revival. As early as 1927 . . . the church called for the commitment of all our energies to the penetration of the life of the nation with the energies of the Gospel. The church acknowledges thankfully the conviction of the leadership of the new Germany, which it shares, that the renewal of people and nation is only possible on the basis of these energies. It is joyfully prepared to play its part in the national and moral renewal of our people.

To carry out this work the church needs complete freedom in the development of its life and work. It trusts the solemn assurance of the government that it will be afforded this freedom.

12 Kapler on the New Church Constitution, 23 April 1933

Dr. Kapler, President of the loose Federation of the twenty-eight provincial churches, tried to forestall 'German Christian' pressure for a new constitution by arranging for the existing church authorities to sponsor a more unitary constitution themselves. The appointment of Müller, with special responsibilities for restructuring the church, made his task more difficult. Friedrich von Bodelschwingh, the highly respected nominee of the churches for the new office of Reich Bishop, was forced to withdraw in favour of Müller, after a commissar had been put in charge of the entire Old Prussian church.

The reform of the constitution of German Protestantism is the dictate of the hour, and must be initiated forthwith. The aim of the reform is the creation of a federal German Evangelical Church, based on, and without prejudice to, the Confession.

17

The off-spring of vigorous provincial churches, it will be accorded all the plenary powers necessary for the fostering of evangelical church life throughout Germany and for representing its interests to people and state at home and abroad.

13 Roman Catholic Conference in Berlin, 25-26 April 1933

The Papacy had been unable to secure from the Weimar state a concordat on terms which it regarded as satisfactory. The advent of the Third Reich, with its advocacy of 'positive Christianity', appeared to present a valuable opportunity to secure better terms, and a distinct threat if cooperation were refused. This conference of diocesan representatives illustrates the hesitations and fears of many of the German Catholics, the political skill of Hitler in allaying them, and the pressure from the Vatican on the German episcopate to come to some accommodation.

. . . Prelate Föhr reports on the visit of the German ministers to Rome. According to his information Papen and Göring left behind a good impression in the Vatican. The discussions are regarded there as a political event of first-class importance. It is desired that nothing should be done to make the relationship between church and state more difficult. The Movement is especially valued because of the struggle against Bolshevism and immorality. The presence of Prelate Kaas in Rome is also valuable. Through him instructions will be given to the Centre Party and the Press . . .

Frau Hessberger, just arrived from Rome, reports to Bishop Berning, who was called out of the conference, that in Rome Prelate Kaas believes that the outlook for the future is very black. All Catholic organisations would be destroyed . . .

Although reassuring explanations as to the maintenance of the confessional school have been given both by the Reich Chancellor and the Minister of Education, strong doubts were uttered as to the reliability of these statements, since the members of the General Teachers Union of Germany, now incorporated in the National Socialist Teachers Association, believe the time has come to force through the unitary school and the non-confessional school. Great fears were also expressed as to the continued existence of the private schools and of the state subsidies . . .

It was also suggested that intercession should be made for those clergy designated as non-Aryan by the laws of the new state, and indeed for all Jewish teachers who had been won over to Catholicism . . .

Outcome of the discussions of the representatives of the episcopate with members of the government:

1. On 25 April Bishop Berning and Bishop Kaller visited the Vice-Chancellor, Herr von Papen. The outcome of this visit is as follows:

Herr von Papen has come to an understanding with Hitler that the freedom of the Catholic church should not be infringed, since a *Kulturkampf* would be fateful for the young state. Göring feels the same. It is expected, on the other hand, that the church will do nothing to conjure up a struggle. The clergy should exercise discretion in their political activities. No prohibition of political activity by the clergy was intended. Nor, for the moment, need there be any fears concerning the Catholic organisations. The lower levels of the NSDAP will certainly be brought to order if they attempt to launch actions against Catholic organisations . . .

In the discussion on this Herr Wolker (General Secretary of the Young Men's Association) who appeared in order to report on the affairs of the youth organisations, said that he distrusted the statements of Herr von Papen, who had discussed with his private secretary, von Savigny, the suppression of the associations. In any event there was a desire to 'de-politicise' them. The problem throughout the whole National Socialist Movement was whether it could cope with the revolutionary masses. A very strong anti-Roman element in the Movement was unmistakable . . .

3. At the request of the conference Bishop Berning, together with General-Vicar Prelate Steinmann, met Reich Chancellor Hitler on 26 April at 2 p.m. The conversation lasted an hour and a quarter. It was friendly and to the point . . .

The bishops recognised joyfully that through the new state Christianity had been promoted, morality improved, and the struggle against Bolshevism and godlessness conducted with energy and success. At the same time the bishops gave expression to the fears which, being widespread among the Catholic population, still hindered a ready cooperation with the state; they requested a definite statement from the Reich Chancellor on the following points:

(1) The freedom of the church seemed threatened by some measures taken in regard to the evangelical church. . . . In certain circles there was anxiety that a *Kulturkampf* might be conjured up.

(2) The question whether the freedom of the Catholic school was in any way threatened . . .

(3) . . . the question whether the Catholic organisations would be able to continue their activities freely and independently, enjoying the same rights as other organisations . . .

(4) The dismissal of civil servants because of their Catholic beliefs, their previous activity in the Centre Party, gives rise to worry and unrest among the Catholic population . . .

Hitler replied in a quiet, factual manner. He had been very eager to have the opportunity to explain his intentions to a Catholic bishop for the first time, since he had frequently been reproached with opposition to Christianity, and the reproach had hurt him deeply! For he was absolutely convinced that neither personal life nor the state could be built up without Christianity; the German state in particular was unthinkable without the firm basis of Christianity, either in the past or in the future . . .

He had been attacked because of the handling of the Jewish question. The Catholic church had regarded the Jews as parasites for 1,500 years, had ushered them into the ghetto, etc.; at that time the Jews had been seen for what they really were. In the era of Liberalism this danger had no longer been seen. I return to the previous period, to what was done for 1,500 years. I do not place race above religion, but I see the representatives of this race as parasites on state and church, and perhaps I am doing Christianity the greatest of services thereby; hence their expulsion from the educational area and the state professions.

My personal attitude to Christianity: I am completely convinced of the great power and the deep importance of the Christian religion and as a consequence will tolerate no other religious founders. For this reason I have turned against Ludendorff and severed my connections with him, for this reason I reject the book by Rosenberg. The book is written by a Protestant. It is not a Party book. It is not written by him as a Party member. Let the Protestants dispute with him about it.

My desire is to prevent any confessional conflict. I must be fair to both confessions. I will tolerate no *Kulturkampf*. There is not the slightest intention of intervening in the church through commissars as happened momentarily in Mecklenburg.

As a Catholic I have no understanding at all for the evangelical church and its structure. Hence I would have great difficulties were I to concern myself with the regulation of the affairs of the Protestant church. The evangelical population or the Protestants would in any case reject him as a Catholic. He stands by his word: I will protect the rights and the freedom of the church and not let them be violated, so that they need have no fears as to the freedom of the church.

The Freedom of the School

A secular school can never be tolerated for this type of school has no religious instruction, and a general instruction in morality without a religious basis is a castle in the air. All up-building of character, all religion, must proceed from faith. From our point of view as representatives of the state we need believing men. In Poland a dark cloud threatens us. We need soldiers, believing soldiers. Believing soldiers are the most valuable. They commit themselves totally. Hence we will maintain the confessional school so that the school may train believing men . . .

Organisations

The Catholic organisations will not be in any way restricted if they carry out their task of furthering the Christian spirit in their members and at the same time have a positive attitude to the state and promote community life. I only resist anything in these organisations which stems perhaps from Liberal or Marxist views and thereby does damage to the state . . .

14 New Guiding Principles of the German Christians, 16 May 1933

The revised guide-lines undoubtedly represent a victory of the more moderate wing—men like Professor Fezer—ι ver the radically racist line championed by Pastor Hosfe nfelder, the Reich Leader of the German Christians. The impatience with out-moded structures in the churches and the idealistic call to service should be noted. With this romantic evocation of a truly German church the German Christians attracted a growing following, especially among the nominally Christian laity.

Aim of the Movement: The national uprising in our fatherland has enabled the German state and the German people to find their way to one another's hearts in a quite new way. It seems

21

now that the German people, reflecting on the deepest sources of its life and energy, wishes also to find its way back to the church. For a German church merely co-existing with the German people is nothing but an empty institution. It will only be a Christian church in the midst of the German people when it is a Church acting on behalf of the German people, helping the German people in selfless service to recognise and carry out its God-given calling . . .

According to the repeated statements of the Chancellor of the Reich this is also the ultimate objective of the present leadership of the nation. This means that it has an entirely different relationship to the church from that state which, in its incredible blindness, regarded life's ultimate truths and deepest energies as of no concern to the state. The new state wants the church. Not to make a pliable tool of her, but because it knows where the foundations of a people are laid. As a result the tasks confronting the church as well as the state have grown stupendously. In their present form the German churches are incapable of carrying out these tasks. The aim of the 'German Christians' is to provide the German churches with a form which will enable them to serve the German people in the specific way the Gospel of Jesus Christ lays upon them for the service of their own people. To achieve this aim we demand:

1. A new church constitution which will appoint the church authorities not by a democratic electoral process, but on the basis of their proven suitability in congregational service;
2. A supreme spiritual authority to take and be responsible for the key decisions;
3. Unification of the evangelical provincial churches into one German Evangelical Church ensuring, however, that special historically based rights will be respected and retained.

We support:

1. The full retention of the confessional basis of the Reformation, insisting, however, on the extension of the Confession to deal decisively with all modern heresies such as mammonism, bolshevism, and unchristian pacifism;
2. The work of the German Evangelical Mission to the Heathen . . . . Recognising the difference between peoples and races as a God-given order for this world, we urge that the cultural heritage of other peoples should not be destroyed by the mission to the heathen . . .
3. The anchoring of the rights and duties of all believers in the church constitution as advocated by Wichern, the father of Home Mission;
4. Sweeping measures to enable our industrious, hard-working and energetic fellow-countrymen and comrades to earn an

22

honest living and found a German-Christian household, in which happiness and blessing will be ensured by the joy of bringing up a merry band of children. The church must also cultivate the spirit of a true, comradely national community, for we are responsible to God not only for ourselves, but also for our neighbours;

5. The resolute extension of Christian charitable work in the church; all business enterprises connected with this must be adequately supervised by the church authorities;

6. Christian schools and an education of all young people to appreciate our debt to our national heritage and our homeland, to steward it faithfully, and to hand it on as a sacred inheritance to the next generation;

7. In short (we support) the church morality of Germany in town and village, Sunday observance, and the nurture of every good, pious, German custom anchored in our race and our cultural heritage.

We pledge ourselves to service in our parishes — and expect this pledge of all Protestant men and women, not just of those in the professional work of the church. We want to serve: by untiring propaganda for our church services; by chivalrous engagement on behalf of the poor and the needy; by the defence of the faith where it is attacked or called in question; by loyal evangelical witness in the secular sphere as well. We want to serve: through our church to serve our God, and thereby our fatherland.

15 Pastoral Counselling in the Third Reich, 28 June 1933

Archbishop Gröber of Freiburg was one of the warmest advocates within the Roman Catholic hierarchy of a positive attitude to the Third Reich. His warning against any criticism of state and Party came at a time when the democratic and legal structures of the Weimar Republic were being systematically dismantled, and Social Democrats and Communists were being hounded unmercifully, not to mention erstwhile members of the Centre Party. Political abstinence by the clergy was to be one of the key clauses in the concordat.

In times like those we are living through now the exercise of the office of preaching and teaching makes increased demands upon the pastor. Even now you will certainly continue to present Catholic teaching in its entirety. You will, however, give particular emphasis to those truths which are conducive to the maintenance of peace and unity, to the consolidation of state authority, and to the spiritual recovery of our people.

We are constrained, in the interests of the pastors themselves and of the church, to add a warning. In preaching, catechising, and religious instruction, as well as in the activities of Catholic organisations and private conversations, anything which could be construed as criticism of the leading personalities in state and community or of the political views they represent should be avoided.

16 Constitution of the German Evangelical Church, 11 July 1933

The new constitution of the German Evangelical Church, although bowing to the German Christian demand for a more unified and centralised church under a Reich Bishop, was a considerable victory for the traditional church authorities, led by Kapler. It insisted on the Reich Bishop acting in close consultation with the provincial churches and, in Article I, defined the church in strongly Scriptural and confessional terms. This article enabled the later Confessing Church to claim that it alone was true to the new constitution.

. . . .

Article 1

The unalterable basis of the German Evangelical Church is the Gospel of Jesus Christ, witnessed to us in Holy Scripture and brought to light again in the Reformation confessions. It is this which defines and delimits the fullness of authority needed by the church for her mission.

Article 2

1. The German Evangelical Church is composed of churches (provincial churches).
3. The provincial churches remain independent in worship and confession.
4. The German Evangelical Church can pass legislation to provide the provincial churches with unitary principles for their constitutions, in so far as these are not confessionally determined . . .
5. Leading office-holders in the provincial churches will be appointed after consultation with the German Evangelical Church.

. . . .

Article 3

1. The German Evangelical Church is in charge of the whole legal life of the German church.
2. It is responsible for its relationship to the state.

. . . .

Article 5

1. At the head of the Church stands the Lutheran Reich Bishop.
2. The Reich Bishop will be advised by a Spiritual Ministry.

. . . .

Article 6

1. The Reich Bishop represents the German Evangelical Church. His task is to give visible expression to the features of church life common to all the provincial churches and to provide a unitary leadership for the work of the German Evangelical Church . . .
2. The Reich Bishop appoints the members of the Spiritual Ministry. He meets regularly with the leading office-holders of the provincial churches for discussion and consultation . . .

. . . .

Article 7

1. The task of the Spiritual Ministry is to govern and to legislate for the German Evangelical Church, under the leadership of the Reich Bishop.
2. It is composed of three theologians and a legal expert . . .

. . . .

Article 8

1. The German Evangelical National Synod is composed of sixty members. Two-thirds are despatched by the German evan-

gelical provincial churches from the synods and church administration. The German Evangelical Church appoints one-third from men with an outstanding record of service to the church.

. . . .

Article 12

1. The Constitution can be altered by legislation, except in regard to the stipulations about confession and worship. The law requires the assent of two-thirds of those attending the National Synod or the unanimous agreement of the Spiritual Ministry.
2. For a constitutional change which has reference to the composition or the administrative organs of the German Evangelical Church, the law requires the participation of the National Synod.

17 Catholic Students Union on National Socialism, 15 July 1933

While Catholic trade-unionists and previous Centre Party officials viewed the National Socialist *gleichschaltung* of Catholic organisations with a jaundiced eye there was little opposition from the professional bodies of the Catholic middle-class. On the other hand, the hysterical enthusiasm of this proclamation by the 'Führer' of the Catholic Students Union was by no means the norm. Students and the universities were overwhelmingly right-wing politically and tended to be unusually sympathetic to the National Socialist revolution.

The Catholic Students Union hails the National Socialist revolution as the great spiritual breakthrough of our time. It is the destiny and the will of the Catholic Students Union to embody and disseminate the idea of the Third Reich . . . and therefore the Catholic Students Union will be led in the National Socialist spirit. . . . Only the powerful National Socialist state, rising out of the Revolution, can bring about for us the re-Christianisation of our culture.

Long live the Catholic Students Union! Long live the Greater German Reich! Heil to our Führer, Adolf Hitler!

18 Völkischer Beobachter on the Church Elections, 19 July 1933

As a result of German Christian agitation, the high-handed actions of August Jäger, the commissar in the Old-Prussian Church, and the refusal of the state to recognise von Bodelschwingh as Reich Bishop, the Protestant churches were in a state of near chaos. This provided the pretext for a sudden proclamation of church elections to resolve the issue and enable the implementation of the new constitution. As this extract from the *Völkischer Beobachter* shows, the NSDAP threw its whole weight behind a massive campaign on behalf of the German Christians.

Attention! Church Elections! Everyone to the polls!
Every Party comrade will carry out his electoral duties on Sunday, 23 July, the day of the church election. That hardly needs to be said. *It is equally obvious that he will give his vote to the 'Faith Movement of German Christians'*. This church election, the first election by the people of the church, is of decisive importance for the future form of the church and for the service it will render the German people. Hence this church election is *no longer an internal church matter*, but a matter for the German people. . . . Every Protestant (man or woman) who is 24 years old on the day of the election is entitled to vote in this present election . . .

19 Radio Broadcast by Hitler on the Church Elections, 22 July 1933

This radio broadcast by Hitler on the eve of the polls made a landslide victory for the German Christians inevitable. An unprecedented intervention in Church affairs, it was a rare error of judgement on Hitler's part. Never again was he to identify himself and the Party with the German Christians.

In making clear what my position is in regard to the evangelical church elections, I am acting purely in my capacity as the political Führer; in other words, the questions of faith, dogmatics, and doctrine are no concern of mine. These are entirely internal church matters. But apart from them there are problems which compel the politician and the responsible Führer of a people to make his position clear. These involve national and state interests in their relationship to the confessions . . .

The strong state must welcome the chance to lend its support to those religious groupings which, for their part, can be useful to it. The evangelical confessions have, in fact, seen the rise of a movement among the church people, the 'German Christians', which is determined to do justice to the great tasks of our time by working for the unification of the evangelical provincial churches and confessions. If this is now a live issue, no manner of stupid or untrue objections will be able to contest the judgement of history that the credit for this lies with the politico-cultural upheaval in Germany and with that movement within the evangelical confessions which clearly and unambiguously declared its solidarity with that national and cultural movement; and this at a time when, alas, just as in the Roman church, countless pastors and superintendents have raised their voices against the national uprising — unjustifiably, polemically, and indeed often fanatically. In the interests of the recovery by the German nation of its former greatness, which I regard as being inseparably bound up with the National Socialist movement, it is understandable that I should wish that the results of the new church elections should assist our new policies for nation and state. Since the state, after all, is prepared to guarantee the inner freedom of religious life, it has a right to hope that within the confessions those forces will gain a hearing which are resolutely determined to make their own contribution to the freedom of the nation. This latter, however, will not be brought about by the unrealistic forces of religious ossification — unable to grasp the importance of contemporary phenomena and events — but only by the enthusiasm of a dynamic movement. This enthusiasm appears to me to be located primarily in that part of the Protestant population which has set itself firmly on the basis of the national socialist state — the German Christians . . .

20 Election Leaflet by Gospel and Church Group, July 1933

The opposition to the German Christians in the church elections of 23 July 1933 was ill-organised, ill-financed and, except in Southern Germany, attracted little support. The emergence of such groups as 'Gospel and Church', however, was significant for the evolution of the Confessing Church. They were sponsored by the Young Reformers Movement, which sought the renewal of the Church, but on a firmly Scriptural and non-political basis. Their bitter opposition to the theology and SA methods of the German Christians should not be confused with any political opposition to the régime.

. . . Our aim is a new form of the church in which the power (of repentance, faith, and brotherly love) is not choked to death by an inflated bureaucracy on the one hand, or by mass movements on the other. We fight for a *free church*. The church must be independent from the state and from the pressure of all political powers. It can only serve the German people as it should if it *declares the Word of God in complete freedom*.

The church of the Gospel is in danger. Hence we summon evangelical Christians to rally around her. Our attitude to our state is one of obedience and love. In this election our *sole* concern is for the church. We want her preaching to be free. We want a renewal from the spirit of God for the service of God. Hence we have joined together with all those who want to fight for a free, young, confessing church. Evangelical Christians, support your church. Church must remain church!

21 Concordat between the Papacy and the Third Reich, 20 July 1933

Everything connected with the concordat is highly controversial. It was, of course, differently regarded by the two parties. The Papacy believed it would provide a permanent, legal basis for church-state relations in Germany. Hitler saw it as a short term political expedient, to neutralise the Centre Party at home and legitimise the Third Reich abroad. In hindsight it is clear that the reality of Catholic organisational strength and political power was sacrificed for the illusion of a legal guarantee. Virtually every clause was to be broken. Moreover the very existence of the concordat fatally compromised Catholic moral resistance to Hitler.

Article 1

The German Reich guarantees freedom of belief and of public worship to the Catholic faith. It recognises the right of the Catholic church — within the limits of the law of the land — to order and administer its own affairs and to make laws and regulations binding upon its members in matters within its competence.

Article 2

The concordats concluded with Bavaria (1924), Prussia (1929), and Baden (1932) remain in force . . .

Article 4

The Holy See enjoys complete freedom in its contacts and its correspondence with the bishops, the clergy and the other members of the Catholic church in Germany. The same holds good for the bishops and other diocesan authorities in their communications with the faithful on all matters concerning their pastoral office . . .

Article 5

The clergy enjoy the protection of the state in the exercise of their spiritual office in the same way as state officials. The state will prosecute insults to their persons . . .

Article 9

Clergy cannot be questioned by judicial or other authorities about facts confided to them in the exercise of their spiritual guidance and which therefore come under the obligation to pastoral confidentiality.

Article 11

The present diocesan organisation and delimitation of the Catholic church in Germany remains in being. . . . The Reich government will approach the Holy See to discuss any reorganisation

of the diocesan organisation and delimitation which may be necessitated by territorial readjustments within the German Reich.

Article 14

As a matter of principle, the church has the right to make its
own appointments to all church offices and benefices, without
the cooperation of the state or of the civic communities . . .
1. Catholic clergy who hold an ecclesiastical office in Germany,
   or exercise pastoral or educational functions, must
(a) be German citizens,
(b) have the qualifications to study at a German institute of
    higher education,
(c) have studied theology and philosophy at least three years in
    a German university, a German ecclesiastical academy, or
    a papal college in Rome.
2. The Bull for the appointment of archbishops, bishops, coad-
   jutors *cum jure successionis* or of a *Praelatus nullius* will not
   be issued until the name of the appointee is submitted to the
   representative of the Reich government in the respective
   province and until it has been ascertained that no objections
   of a general political nature exist . . .

Article 15

Monastic orders and religious associations . . . are not subject
to any special restrictions by the state . . .

Article 16

Before bishops enter upon the government of their dioceses they
are to take an oath of fealty either to the representative of the
Reich government in the provinces or to the president of the
Reich in the following words: 'Before God and on the Holy Gos-
pels I swear and promise — as becomes a bishop — loyalty to the
German Reich and to the . . . state. I swear and promise to
honour the constitutional government and to cause the clergy of
my diocese to honour it. In the exercise of the spiritual office
entrusted to me I will endeavour, with due solicitude for the
well-being and the interests of the German state, to prevent any
harm which might threaten it.'

Article 19

The Catholic theological faculties in the universities will remain
in being . . .

Article 21

Instruction in the Catholic faith is a regular part of the curric-
ulum in the elementary, technical, intermediate, and high schools

and is taught in accordance with the principles of the Catholic church. It will be a special concern of religious instruction, as is the case with all other subjects, to inculcate a sense of patriotic, civic, and social duty in the spirit of Christian faith and morality. The syllabus and selection of text-books for religious instruction will be determined with the agreement of the church authorities . . .

Article 23

The retention and establishment of Catholic confessional schools is guaranteed . . .

Article 26

Without prejudice to a comprehensive regulation of the marriage laws at a later stage, there is agreement that the religious ceremony can precede the civil marriage, except in a case when the critical illness of one of the partners does not permit any delay, or in the case of grave moral necessity, whose existence must be certified by the episcopal authority concerned. In such cases the pastor is obliged to inform the registrar's office at once.

Article 27

Special pastoral provision will be made for the Catholic officers, officials, and men of the German army, together with their families.

The pastoral care for the army will be under the oversight of the Army Bishop. The Holy See will appoint him to his church office, after consultation with the Reich government has secured its approval for a suitable candidate.

The Army Bishop will be responsible for the church appointment of military chaplains and other military clergy after gaining the consent of the relevant Reich authority . . .

Article 30

On Sundays and recognised holy days prayer will be made for the well-being of the German Reich and people . . .

Article 31

The property and activities of those Catholic organisations and associations whose aims are purely religious, cultural, or charitable and which, therefore, are under the authority of the hierarchy, will be protected.

Catholic organisations which pursue other aims, social or professional, for example, as well as religious, cultural, or charitable, will, without prejudice to any possible incorporation into state associations, come under the protection of the first paragraph of Article 31 in so far as they guarantee that their activity is outwith the orbit of any political party.

The enumeration of the organisations and associations covered by the terms of this article will be a matter to be agreed upon jointly by the Reich government and the German episcopate.

Care will be taken that the members of any sporting or other youth organisations controlled by the Reich or the provincial governments will be able to take a regular part in their church duties on Sundays and feast days, and that nothing incompatible with their religious and moral convictions and duties will be urged upon them.

Article 32

In view of the peculiar situation in Germany and the assurances given by the terms of the above concordat of a legislative basis for the rights and freedoms of the Catholic church in the Reich and its provinces, the Holy See will issue regulations to prohibit clergy and members of monastic orders from membership in political parties or activity on behalf of such parties.

Article 33

. . . Should differences of opinion arise in future as to the interpretation or application of any of the terms of the concordat the Holy See and the German Reich will consult together to resolve the matter in a friendly manner.

The Supplementary Protocol
. . . .

Article 32

It is understood that similar provisions prohibiting participation in politics will be made by the Reich for members of the non-Catholic confessions.

The conduct required of clergy and members of the monastic orders under Article 32 does not mean any limitation of the duty to preach and interpret the dogmatic and moral teachings and principles of the church.

22 Ratification of the Concordat, 10 September 1933

In view of the failure to reach agreement on the interpretation of the crucial clause 31 and the increasing harassment of Catholic organisations, the question whether the concordat should be ratified was more than a mere formality. This letter by Cardinal Bertram to Pacelli, State Secretary of the Vatican, written on 2 September, shows that the German hierarchy clung to the view that speedy ratification was the only way to secure an effective legal basis for their protests. Despite the evident National Socialist contempt for legality they believed that there was enough in common between Catholicism and National Socialism (anti-Communism, anti-materialism) to ensure a relatively harmonious coexistence.

A retardation of the ratification of the Reich Concordat is not recommended. On the contrary, for the following reasons it is desirable that the ratification take place very soon.
1. From many quarters voices are being raised against the concordat. Even voices which assert that the Reich Chancellor is simply pursuing a diplomatic success for prestige reasons without any whole-hearted desire for its implementation on the home front.
2. It is being said quite widely that the government has gone too far in its concessions; that a move in the opposite direction would be desirable. Such voices will become louder if ratification is delayed. This disturbs the Catholic population.
3. We will only be able to take more decisive action against the countless anti-Catholic actions after ratification . . .
On the other hand it is highly desirable that an end to the grievances be demanded at the same time as ratification is effected . . .
It is admittedly impossible to dissipate all doubts about the meaning and the scope of all the clauses of the concordat. That must be left to the future. Reference, however, can be made here to the following current grievances:
1. Relating to the Catholic organisations, especially the Youth and Young Men's Associations and the Workers Associations.
   i Right up to the present moment innumerable assaults have been made in every region of Germany on the property, the premises, and the equipment of Catholic organisations. Their funds, too, have been confiscated . . .
   ii On all sides Catholic associations are publicly slandered, being accused of political unreliability, of lack of patriotism, of enmity against the state. They are denounced for hindering the unitary drive of the totalitarian state by involving the German people in confessional rivalries. For this reason, it is said, they have no place in the new Reich.

. . . All associations whose individual members previously tended to belong to the Centre Party are suspect, and doubt is cast upon their loyalty to the new Reich . . .

iii Everywhere individual members of the Catholic associations are under great pressure. They are discriminated against in all branches of economic life. As a result they are justifiably afraid that their careers and their families will suffer. . . . According to reports from all over the country everyone who is not a Party comrade of National Socialism is dismissed, every young person who does not belong to the 'Hitler Youth' . . .

Parents no longer want to let their children belong to Catholic organisations because membership appears to threaten the future of the children. Countless resignations from the Catholic organisations everywhere because of pressure from the subordinate organs of the National Socialist Party which are not effectively restrained by the higher authorities.

iv . . . Everywhere teachers are under pressure to direct children to the Hitler Youth. The teachers have to report on their success in this under threat of dismissal or a prejudicial transfer. Thus the living reservoirs for the Catholic associations are being cut off . . .

v There are countless cases of the activities and meetings of the Catholic Youth organisations and Young Men's associations being kept under the closest watch. They are unfavourably regarded and not infrequently prevented from taking place. The Catholic associations are often forbidden to engage in sport, hiking, public rallies, to hold meetings or recruiting campaigns . . .

vi A painful impression is made by the prohibition on Hitler Youth members belonging at the same time to a Catholic organisation. This deprives the young people in the non-Catholic organisations of the blessed influence which should be infused into their hearts by contact with the spirit of the Catholic organisations.

2. The Struggle for the Catholic Press

i Catholic newspapers are forbidden to describe themselves as 'Catholic'. . . . There should, it is said, no longer be a Catholic Press, but only a German Press.

ii Such papers as remains have not the right to state their views freely. If articles appear which are suspected by the Press police of passing an unfavourable judgement on state measures the paper is forbidden for weeks or months. . . . Censorship of content, tone, and all editorial opinion is very severe . . .

iv A check is kept among workers and other similar groups to see whether they are subscribing to the National Socialist newspaper. Since very few can afford to take two papers this helps to edge out the Catholic Press.

. . . .

4. Will it be possible for the Holy See to put in a warm-hearted word for those who have been converted from Judaism to the Christian religion, since either they themselves, or their children or grandchildren, are now facing a wretched fate because of their lack of Aryan descent? . . .

23 Circular Letter by Niemöller, 21 September 1933

The success of the German Christians at the July elections put much of the church structures—synods, executive councils, administrations—into their hands. On the level of congregational life, on the other hand, of 'the praying and worshipping people', unease grew at the character of the men in charge of their church. As Ludwig Müller was appointed bishop of the Old-Prussian Church by the 'Brown Synod' of 5 September, a leader of real genius emerged on the other side, Pastor Martin Niemöller. His Pastors Emergency Alliance rallied opposition around loyalty to Scripture and the Confessions. Significantly, the pledge its members took rejected any application of the 'Aryan clause' to the pastorate.

(a)
At the recent meeting of the Prussian General Synod the German-Christian majority forced through a series of laws changing the constitution. The objections of the minority, which were based at least partly on the church's confessional nature, were not met; a thorough preparation or even a discussion of the matter in committee was not permitted.

On the day after the General Synod six General Superintendents were dismissed from office and retired without any sort of explanation. Since this time there has been widespread confusion, perplexity, and deep unrest among the congregations in and around Berlin. This state of affairs is aggravated by stormy goings-on in some congregations. Church organisations, for example, which do not want to lend their wholehearted support to the 'Faith Movement of German Christians' are forbidden the use of the rooms in the church house on the instructions of the congregation's church council. In other instances, specific measures have been taken against individual pastors at the behest of the 'Faith Movement' in their respective congregations, the goal being 'disciplinary removal'. Characteristically, the church 'leaders' and authorities have capitulated to these endeavours, since the people now demand that the promise given in the election campaign should now be kept.

These events have given rise to a shameful faint-heartedness among many ministerial brethren; although serious-minded men, some have even gone over to the 'German Christians' against their own better judgement, knowing that what they did was contrary to their ordination vow and was a violation of their consciences.

Because of this distress we have called into being an 'Emergency Alliance' of pastors who have given one another their word in a written declaration that they will be bound in their preaching by Holy Scripture and the Reformation confessions alone (hence to no 'bond' or any other 'spiritual' authority) and that they will alleviate the distress of those brethren who have to suffer for this to the best of their ability.

Support has been solicited privately by trusted individuals; as a result the whole membership of the Young Reformers Movement has not yet been reached. At the moment about 1,300 have signed, not counting Westphalia which already had its own fraternity. Members of the Young Reformers Movement who wish to join an alliance of this nature are cordially invited to request from me the engagement to membership.

Our aim must be to have an alliance like this in every provincial church and every province; that these alliances should stand by one another (otherwise one province will be 'cleaned up' after the other); and that the members of the alliance actively set about building up the Christian congregation within their sphere of influence (mobilisation of the laity).

I am well aware that this alliance will neither redeem the church nor shake the world; but I am equally aware that we owe it to the Lord of the church and to the brethren to do what we can; in these days a prudent retreat to the role of a mere spectator amounts to betrayal, for those under stress have no assurance of our brotherly solidarity. So let us act!

In brotherly solidarity,
Your Niemöller

(b)
1. I pledge myself to exercise my office as a servant of the Word under the sole authority of Holy Scripture and the confessions of the Reformation as the correct interpretation of Holy Scripture.
2. I pledge myself to protest against any violation of this confessional stance with all the strength at my command.
3. I recognise my responsibility to do all in my power for those who suffer persecution because of this confessional stance.
4. Acting on this responsibility I testify that with the application of the Aryan paragraph to the realm of the church of Christ the confessional stance has been violated.

24 Rudolf Hess on the religious allegiance of Party Members, 17 October 1933

Ludwig Müller, elected Reich Bishop by the National Synod in Wittenberg (27 September 1933), was apparently at the height of his power. Already, however, its threadbare character was becoming apparent. The continual uproar caused by his tactics was reported assiduously by the international Press and caused the new régime considerable diplomatic embarrassment. Moreover the German Christians' virtual identification of the Party's cause with their own threatened the supra-confessional appeal of the latter. Hess, Hitler's deputy, very firmly rejects any such identification here. This was ominous, for the real and only reason for the German Christian successes had been the support of the NSDAP.

In connection with the statement by the Reich Bishop Müller that no pastor will be discriminated against because he does not belong to the Faith Movement of the 'German Christians', I decree as follows:

No National Socialist may be discriminated against in any way for not adhering to a particular type of belief or confession or for not belonging to any confession at all.

Belief is an individual, absolutely personal affair for which one is responsible only to one's own conscience.

No pressure may be brought to bear in matters of conscience.

25 The 'Sports Palace Scandal', 13 November 1933

This sensational address by Dr. Krause, the leader of the Berlin German Christians, triumphantly acclaimed by an audience of some 20,000 people which included Bishop Hossenfelder and other leading dignitaries of the German Christians, marked the beginning of the end of the 'Faith Movement'. Krause resigned from office forthwith but it proved impossible to dissociate the German Christians from Krause's wild utterances. Resignations from moderate German Christians poured in, Krause formed a splinter group of his own, and the initiative passed into the hands of the fast-growing Emergency Alliance of Niemöller.

What Protestants really wanted was not so much a new constitution for the church or new church authorities but the completion of the national mission of Martin Luther by a second German Reformation. This will result not in an authoritarian, clergy-dominated church, but rather in a church for the German people, a church able to accommodate the whole breadth of a racially attuned experience of God. In its outward form, too, it will be structured in the truly German manner to be expected in the Third Reich. (Very loud applause)

Can our Reich church, our provincial church, achieve this? Only, my evangelical compatriots, if it renounces all violation of religious life, and turns its back on any 'Christianity on command'. The first priority is to win over the flood of those who are returning to the church. This requires a feeling for the homeland, and the first step towards the church becoming at home in Germany is the liberation from all that is un-German in liturgy and confession, liberation from the Old Testament with its Jewish recompense ethic, from all these stories about cattle-dealers and pimps. This book has been characterised quite rightly as one of the most questionable books in the world's history. It just will not do for German Christians pastors to explain: 'We stand where we have always stood — on the basis of the Old Testament', although, on the other hand, the guiding principles speak of 'racially attuned Christianity'. In practice the one excludes the other.

. . . Our provincial church will also have to see to it that all obviously distorted and superstitious reports should be expunged from the New Testament, and that the whole scape-goat and inferiority-type theology of the Rabbi Paul should be renounced

39

in principle, for it has perpetrated a falsification of the Gospel, of the simple message: 'Love your neighbour as yourself' — regard your neighbour as your brother and God as your father. The fact is that the whole history of the development of dialectical theology from Paul to Barth has made a speculative exercise out of our God-Father. Theology has always tried to separate God and man, tried again and again to justify its own existence by proving that man is fallen, weighed down with original sin, and therefore in need of the salvation the church can offer. We recognise no God/man division, except when man deliberately sets himself apart from God . . .

26 Treaty between the Reich Bishop and the Hitler Youth, 19 December 1933

The Evangelical Youth, with some 700,000 members in various Protestant organisations, had been strongly influenced by National Socialist ideas. On 17 September 1933 it entrusted the Reich Bishop with personal executive authority over it. Müller abused these powers by negotiating its integration with the Hitler Youth on terms which effectively destroyed the character of the church youth organisations. Opposition from the latter was met by a wave of terrorist actions and the storm of protest led by Bishops Wurm of Württemberg and Meiser of Bavaria only abated when it became evident that the State would ratify the treaty. The Pastors Emergency Alliance, however, continued to protest. The following statement, signed by Müller and by von Schirach, Youth Leader of the Third Reich, indicates how the treaty was to be implemented in practice.

1. The Evangelical Youth recognises that the whole political education of the German youth is carried out by the National Socialist state and the Hitler Youth as the representatives of the secular arm. Members of the Evangelical Youth under the age of 18 will be incorporated into the Hitler Youth and its subordinate groupings. From now on no one in this age-group can be a member of the Evangelical Youth unless he is a member of the Hitler Youth.

2. Athletic (including gymnastic and sporting) and political training up to the age of 18 will be pursued only in the Hitler Youth.
3. All members of the Evangelical Youth will . . . wear the uniform of the Hitler Youth.
4. The Evangelical Youth retains full freedom for its activities in educational and church matters . . . on two afternoons in the week and on two Sundays in the month. On these days the members will where necessary be released from the other oganisation. For Evangelical Youth members service in the Hitler Youth will likewise be restricted to two afternoons and two Sundays. Members of the Evangelical Youth will also be exempted from service in the Hitler Youth to enable them to attend missionary courses and camps for evangelical training and education.

27 The 'Muzzling Decree', 4 January 1934

1933 ended with the Protestant churches in a state of uproar. Widespread calls for Müller's resignation followed the surrender of the Evangelical Youth. His only answer was a clumsy attempt to gag all discussion in the still relatively free realm of the church. To add insult to injury the decree of 4 January also reinstated the 'Aryan paragraph', which had been suspended on 16 November 1933. An unprecedented flood of protests from church leaders and theology faculties was the result. The members of the Pastors Emergency Alliance read out from their pulpits a statement rejecting the decree. Many, including Niemöller himself, were suspended from office, others fined, imprisoned, or transferred.

The controversies about church politics are destroying the peace and retarding the unification of the church; they undermine the necessary bond between the evangelical church and the National Socialist state, thereby endangering both the proclamation of the Gospel and the newly-won national unity.

In order to safeguard the constitution of the German Evangelical Church and to restore orderly conditions I therefore, without prejudice to any future measures, and in responsible exercise

41

of the office of Führer which is my constitutional right under Article 6, par. I of the Constitution of the German Evangelical Church, decree the following:

1. The church service is for the proclamation of the pure Gospel, and for this alone. The misuse of the church service for controversies about church politics, in whatever form, has to cease. The release or use of churches or other church premises for any kind of meetings about church politics is forbidden.
2. Any one holding office in the church who circulates publications, especially pamphlets and circulars, directed against the leadership of the church or its constitution or who attacks them in public is in breach of the duties attached to his office . . .
3. Any one holding office in the church who contravenes the stipulations of paragraphs 1 and 2 will be automatically suspended from office and a formal disciplinary process will be initiated immediately with the aim of removing him from office . . .

. . . .

28 Hitler Receives the Protestant Church Leaders, 25 January 1934

Since the July elections some provincial churches, especially in the North, had German Christian leaders; others, the so-called 'intact churches', like Württemberg and Bavaria, were led by men loyal to Scripture and the Reformation confessions (referred to as 'our party' in this report by Bishop Wurm). Hitler summoned both parties to an 'audience' in which he intervened once again to urge support for Müller. He used an indiscretion by Niemöller (representing the Emergency Alliance) to detach the Southern Lutherans from him, and relied, for the rest, on patriotic appeals and a profession of his Protestant sympathies (!) to secure a promise of renewed loyalty to Müller.

The audience began with the reading of a telegram which Göring had received from the political police. According to this Niemöller had made the following remark about the Reich President's reception of the Reich Chancellor that same morning: 'The Reich President will give the Reich Chancellor the necessary directions for the solution of the church conflict; the position in regard to the Ministry for the Interior also seemed to be favourable. Hindenburg will give Hitler 'extreme unction'; if the worst comes to the worst one can take the leap into a Free church.'

Niemöller at once acknowledged that the report was in substance correct; as he later made plain, the phrase 'extreme unction' was not his. He tried to explain the nature of the conversation by reference to the strain the Pastors Emergency Alliance had been under for months in its struggle for the maintenance of the church's confession, and stressed that this struggle was not directed *against* the Third Reich, but that it, too, was *for the sake of* this Reich.

Hitler countered very sharply that concern for the Third Reich should be left to him; this interpretation of his audience with the Reich President had deprived him of any freedom of decision. Even if he had been disposed to distance himself from the person of the present Reich Bishop methods such as these had the opposite effect of driving him to his side. It was undeniable that in many cases Protestant pastors were whipping up feeling against the government and against National Socialism. To prove this he had Minister-President Göring read out a series of reports by the political police on sermons and articles in the church press which contained such utterances.

In a passionate tone the Chancellor complained that this conflict in the evangelical church, because of its exploitation by the foreign Press, made the position of the Third Reich much more difficult. Prior to its victory many evangelical pastors had been opponents of the Movement. He had tried to help the church forward, as it had to a large degree lost touch with the masses of the people; if it were incapable of exploiting the opportunity, he would withdraw his hand — in financial matters as well.

He had not forced Müller on us, but we could not drop him after only four months, but should make another real attempt to co-operate with him. He himself had been born a Catholic. He was thankful to destiny for this, since it had enabled him to win millions of Catholics, too, to National Socialism. Inwardly he stood closer to the Evangelical church, but also expected of it a different attitude to that of the Catholics.

The church leaders of our group emphasised that isolated expressions of political discontent could not be urged as evidence of reactionary sentiments among the pastorate as a whole. Our struggle was devoted solely to the purification of the church from false teaching and incapable leadership; the Reich Bishop showed no evidence of possessing the necessary qualities of leadership and had also laid himself open to ridicule by his conduct of business and his public utterances.

The Reich Chancellor replied inter alia that nothing was more liable to precipitate a fierce struggle than the transfer of the leadership of the church to a man who enjoyed our confidence. We might have the conservative sections of the population and the majority of the 'priests' behind us, but a revolution was taking place in the church, too, and he had a prophetic eye for what would happen if we did not come to terms with these new forces. Only a man with the confidence of the Movement could have the leadership of the church.

Over against this it was pointed out that there were large areas which were both loyal to the church and in favour of National Socialism, and yet devoid of support for the 'German Christians'.

The representatives of the other group among the church leaders denied that they propagated heretical views and argued that the whole conflict was purely on the question of church order, not about questions of confession or the nature of the church. The Reich Chancellor concluded with an urgent appeal to join forces in a Christian and brotherly way with the Reich Bishop and so end the conflict which, because of the political situation, could no longer be tolerated. At this point the Reich Bishop announced that he would invite the church leaders to a joint discussion about the formation of a new 'Spiritual Ministry' . . .

29 The Dismissal of Bishop Wurm, 15 April 1934

1934 saw a series of attempts to destroy the independence of the various provincial churches and concentrate power in the hands of the Reich Bishop. This was, of course, in line with the general National Socialist *gleichschaltung* of cultural life. In the case of the churches, however, popular bishops like Wurm were able to mobilise instant grassroots support where traditional teachings and institutions were threatened. After the service at which this statement was read out the congregation gathered on the square in front of the Stuttgart Stiftskirche, singing in protest "Ein feste Burg", the defiant hymn of Luther. The bungling attempt to dismiss Wurm only rallied the church within Württemberg and outside it behind him. The Ulm Agreement of

22 April 1934 prepared the way for a nation-wide alliance of the Southern 'confessing churches' with the 'confessing synods' which were springing up spontaneously in the German Christian provinces of the North.

I am informed that the following statement was made on the radio yesterday evening: 'The committee of the Württemberg Provincial Synod has decided to withdraw its support from the provincial bishop. The accusation levelled by his congregations is that the conduct of the provincial bishop has provoked disquiet among the people; above all, his relations with the notorious Pastors Emergency Alliance have met with incomprehension. As a result there now exists a state of emergency in the Württemberg church. Bishop Wurm is no longer an acceptable public figure in the new Reich. The representatives of the Reich in the province has been compelled to call upon the Reich Bishop to deal with the emergency. The Reich Bishop will be in Stuttgart by tomorrow.'

In reply I would like to point out that there has been no meeting of the standing committee of the Provincial Synod at which such a decision could have been taken. A meeting has been convened for 5 p.m. today by the Reich Bishop. Whether it will come to this decision remains to be seen. The constitution of the Württemberg church stipulates that the bishop can only be dismissed by a two-thirds majority of a plenary meeting of the provincial synod. Right up to the present time the overwhelming majority of the pastors of the province, backed by their congregations, have consistently expressed their confidence in the provincial bishop. Hence the assumption that the provincial bishop is no longer acceptable to the evangelical congregations is scarcely accurate. (He has so often demonstrated his positive attitude to the Third Reich that this reproach, too, must be repudiated).

For the sake of our church, and not for my own sake, I will not recognise a forcible dismissal of this sort. . . . It would be gratifying if the true feeling of the church people were to be expressed at the congregational level . . .

30 The Barmen Synod, 29-31 May 1934

Its way prepared by various provincial synods, Barmen was a quite remarkable event for German Protestantism, hitherto weakened by bitter rivalries between Lutheran, Reformed, and United Churches. The new-found unity, owing much to the theology of Barth and the determination of Niemöller, but perhaps still more to the follies of Müller, was forged in the firm conviction that it was the work not of man, but of God. The very structure of each article— Biblical authority, positive teaching, negative canon—illustrates the priority it sought to give to Scriptural theology. Its aim was not to found a rival church to that of the German Christians but to gather together the one true church of Christ in Germany, on the basis of the July 1933 Constitution.

Theological Statement Concerning the Present Position of the German Evangelical Church.

. . . .

We, the representatives of Lutheran, Reformed, and United Churches, of free synods, church assemblies, and congregational groupings, gathered together as the Confessing Synod of the German Evangelical Church, declare that we take as our common basis the German Evangelical Church as a federation of the German Confessing Churches . . .

. . . .

The false teachings of the German Christians and of the present Reich Church Government are wreaking havoc in the church and thereby disrupting the unity of the German Evangelical Church. In view of this we bear witness to the following evangelical truths:

1. "I am the way, the truth, and the life: no man cometh unto the Father but by me." (John 14, 6)

   "Verily, verily, I say unto you, He that entereth not by the door into the sheepfold, but climbeth up some other way, the same is a thief and a robber. I am the door; by me if any man enter in, he shall be saved." (John 10, 1, 9)

   Jesus Christ, as witnessed to us in Holy Scripture, is the one word of God to which we have to listen, trust, and obey in life and in death.

   We reject the false teaching that the church can and must recognise any other events, powers, personalities, and truths apart from and in addition to this one word of God as sources of its proclamation.

2.

. . . .

   We reject the false teaching that there are areas of our life which are subject not to Jesus Christ, but to other lords, areas in which justification and sanctification through him are not needful.

3.
. . . .

We reject the false teaching that the church can let the form
of its message and its polity be determined by its own incli-
nations or by the ideological or political views which happen
to have the upper hand at the time.

. . . .
5.
. . . .

We reject the false teaching that the state has the right or the
power to exceed its own particular remit and become the sole
and total authority in human life thus fulfilling the task of
the church as well.

. . . .

Statement on the Legal Position of the Confessing Synod of
the German Evangelical Church.
1. The unalterable basis of the German Evangelical Church is
the Gospel of Jesus Christ, witnessed to us in Holy Scripture
and brought to light again in the Reformation confessions.

The present Reich Church Government has departed from
this unalterable basis and has committed countless breaches
of the law and of the constitution. Thereby it has forfeited
its right to be the legitimate leadership of the German Evangelical Church.

. . . .

31 Proscription of the Jehovah's Witnesses, 11 June 1934

The determined internationalism of the Jehovah's Witnesses and their uncompromising opposition to the claims
of any state, not to mention a totalitarian one, led the Party
to suspect a sinister conspiracy behind their rejection of
civic duties and military service and behind their apocalyp-
tic language, a Bolshevist ideology. Apart from the Jews
no religious body met with such systematic persecution.
Virtually every single member suffered, and many were ex-
ecuted or died in a concentration camp.

The International Bible Students Union, together with its sub-sidiary organisations, is prohibited in accordance with par. 1 of the decree of the Reich President for the Protection of People and State of 28 February 1933. . . . This has been necessitated by the agitation of the Jehovah's Witnesses against the institutions of church and state . . .

32 SS Report on Catholic Clergy, May/June 1934

This is a very brief extract from a fifty-page secret report on the religious bodies in the Reich circulated by Himmler as head of the SS. By this time few members of the Catholic clergy had been unaffected by the constant pressure and restrictions on Catholic organisations, newspapers, and schools. Faulhaber is a good example of the patriotic, right-wing, even to a degree anti-Semitic cleric who found himself increasingly at odds with the National Socialist state. His famous sermons at the end of 1933 defended the Old Testament (not Judaism!), and attacked the blood and soil ideology as anti-Christian.

. . . .

Munich: Cardinal Faulhaber is generally regarded as the in-tellectual leader of Catholic resistance to the National Socialist state, especially in the foreign Press. . . . His occasional exhor-tations to the clergy that they should 'co-operate with the state' . . . are eclipsed by the disruptive effects of his Advent sermons on Judaism and in particular by his sermon on New Year's Eve about Germanism. While the Advent sermons may perhaps be understandable as a reaction to attacks on the Old Testament, the statements made about Germanism were without scientific basis and can only be characterised as a political misuse of the pulpit, especially when they were taken as the theme for a New Year's Eve service. The sermons attracted huge attendances, and in book form they sold like hot cakes . . .
. . . .
Hostile Clergy
. . . .
The most dangerous activity of countless Catholic clergy is the way in which they 'mope about', spreading despondency. Fa-

48

vourite topics are the 'dangers of a new time', 'the present emergency', 'the gloomy future'. Prophecies are made about the speedy downfall of National Socialism or at the very least mention is made of the transience of all political phenomena, compared with the Catholic Church which will outlive them all. National Socialist achievements and successes are passed over in silence.

There is thus a deliberate undermining of the very basis of the National Socialist programme of reconstruction, the people's trust in the leadership of the state.

. . . .

33 The Dahlem Synod, 20 October 1934

For a Protestantism accustomed to operate in the closest cooperation with the state the decision taken at Dahlem to set up an 'emergency' church government, based on congregational and synodal support, was a momentous step. It appears to be the sole example of a major public body being established after 1933 against the wishes of state and Party. This radical step, however, had only been taken under the impression of further attempts to incorporate the South German Lutheran churches. When pressure on the latter decreased they tended to fall back on a provincial confessionalism. The strongest support for the new Provisional Leadership and its Fraternal Council came from the Prussian North.

The Reich Church Government has now followed up the dismissal of the church leadership of Electoral Hesse with that of Württemberg and Bavaria. This has brought to a head the chaotic situation within the evangelical church which has been evident since the summer of 1933. In view of this we feel constrained to make the following statement:

I

1. The first and fundamental article of the Constitution of the German Evangelical Church . . . has been, in effect, swept aside by the teachings, laws, and actions of the Reich Church Government. The Christian basis of the German Evangelical Church has thus been nullified.

49

2. The National Church pursued by the Reich Bishop under the slogan 'one state — one people — one church' means that the Gospel is debarred from the German Evangelical Church and that the church's message is surrendered to the powers of this world.

3. The sole sovereignty which the Reich Bishop and his Legal Administrator have presumed to take upon themselves has erected a Papal hegemony unthinkable within the evangelical church.

4. Propelled forward by the spirit of a false, unbiblical revelation the Church Government has punished obedience to Scripture and Confession as an offence against discipline.

5. The unscriptural introduction of the secular Führer principle into the church and the consequent demand for unconditional obedience has bound those who hold office in the church to the church government instead of to Christ.

6. The elimination of the synods has silenced the congregations and robbed them of their rights in contradiction to the biblical and Reformation teaching of the priesthood of all believers.

II

1. All the protests, warnings, and exhortations we have made on the basis of Scripture and Confession have been in vain. Indeed, the Reich Church Government has ruthlessly gone on destroying the church, invoking the authority of the Führer and drawing on the co-operation of political powers.

2. The rape of the South German churches has taken from us the last hope that by working from within the situation order can be restored to the church.

3. This means that we have to proclaim today that a state of emergency exists and that the church has the right to act in order to remedy it.

III

1. We must conclude, therefore, that the constitution of the German Evangelical Church has collapsed. Its legitimate authorities no longer exist. The men who have taken into their hands the leadership of the church in the Reich and the provinces have behaved in a manner which cuts them off from the Christian church.

2. The Confessing Synod of the German Evangelical Church sets up new organs of leadership on the basis of the right of those churches, congregations, and holders of spiritual office who are bound to Scripture and Confession to act in this emergency situation. It appoints the Fraternal Council of the German Evangelical Church to lead and to represent the

German Evangelical Church as a federation of confessionally bound churches. The Council of the German Evangelical Church, whose membership is drawn from the Fraternal Council, will be responsible for the conduct of business. The membership and constitution of both organs takes account of the different confessions.

3. We call upon the Christian congregations, pastors, and elders to accept no instructions from the previous Reich Church Government and its authorities and to withdraw all co-operation from those who intend to continue rendering this Church Government their obedience. We call upon them to abide by the instructions of the Confessing Synod of the German Evangelical Church and of its recognised organs.

IV

We submit this declaration of ours to the Reich Government, requesting it to take note of the decision which has been taken, and demanding from it the recognition that in matters which pertain to the church, to its doctrine and its good order, the church alone — without prejudice to the state's right of supervision — has the right to judge and to decide. Berlin — Dahlem, 20 October, 1934.

The Confessing Synod of the German
Evangelical Church
D. Koch, Präses.

34 The Gestapo and the Churches, 12 November 1934 & 6 May 1935

The directives sent out by the Bavarian Political Police on 12 November 1934 and 6 May 1935 are early examples of the largely successful policy of sealing off the Confessing Church within a communications ghetto, after the failure of Müller's attempt at overt suppression.

(i) With reference to the Protestant Church Struggle:

The Reich Minister of Internal Affairs has issued the following decree on 6/11/34 under Nr. VI 7770/3014:

'Recently there have been an increasing number of instances

of unseemly reports about matters relating to the Protestant Church reaching the public. Until further notice I forbid all publications dealing with the Protestant Church in the daily press, in pamphlets, and in leaflets, with the exception of official statements of the Reich Church Government.'

A supplementary decree of the R.M. of I.A. of 7/11/34 also prohibits publications about the present situation of the Protestant Church in Germany in church newspapers, weekly papers, congregational news-sheets, and periodicals.

In order to bring about a lasting religious pacification of the populace and to secure public stability, order, and security these edicts should be enforced with all possible rigour . . .

(ii) With reference to measures against activity hostile to the state:

Recently the clergy of both Christian confessions have been displaying more and more openly and actively their hostility to state interests. In order to suppress behaviour so detrimental to the state, local authorities will have to step up their supervision of the clergy's conduct. Extreme care, however, must be taken to avoid under all circumstances any interruption of the cultic activities of the Churches.

. . . .

35 German Faith, 1934

Various attempts were made at this period to find in Germanism a viable alternative to the Christian faith. The most considerable of these was Hauer's German Faith Movement. The extracts from his book *The German Vision of God (Deutsche Gottschau)* illustrate the extravagant mixture of pantheism and romanticism in which he indulged. His attacks on the 'obscurantism' of traditional Christianity were sincerely enough meant, but were cynically exploited by the NSDAP for its own ends. Despite its anti-semitism and adulation of Hitler his movement was never allowed to become a rival to the Party itself.

We contend for faith against all un-faith. But faith is not the intellectual belief that something is true. Faith is life, is strength, is the most profound certainty. In faith we encounter eternal reality, in whose company we are joyful and resolute. Hence faith is commitment to the will of this reality, is activity and battle under its imperative, is the knowledge that it will be victorious. It is a confidence in the power which dwells in the heart, where the God of action joins himself to the man of integrity, the man prepared for sacrifice . . .

Within us surges the power of a new passionate emotion, dynamic life from the holy depths of *our people*, the source of all historic greatness within the German realm; we are swept away by a love, the love for our people's eternal being, from which the very word 'faith' itself was once born.

Why *German* faith? . . . *'German'* has the meaning of 'wedded to the soil', 'true to type'. Since we stand on German soil, are rooted in German life and blood, the term 'German Faith' arose naturally from our struggle . . . for the German people . . .

We are thankful for every great man in the Western Indo-Germanic area, although outside the political boundaries of Germany, whose life and creativity have the same basis as the great Germans: for a Dante, a Giordano Bruno, a Michelangelo and Shakespeare, a Björnson and Ibsen. They belong to us, belong to the 'German' realm just as much as the Edda and the Nordic sagas, because their life springs from the same blood and the same spirit as ours; for the original meaning of 'German', after all, throughout this whole area, is 'belonging to the people', to that people — in the broadest sense of the word — to which fate has assigned this area. When we speak of a German faith, the line of demarcation we are drawing is over against an alien type of culture and not against other peoples in this area of a similar kind to ourselves . . .

. . . .

With the World War and the *German Revolution the faith of the German man has taken an elemental turn towards the present*. Paradoxically it is in these grave and difficult times that he has won through to a trust in the immediate present, to an awareness of the presence of God in the contemporary events of his life. This turning towards the present exorcizes for him the danger of religious historicism, even in the field of German Faith. His eyes are not turned back to the past. He looks resolutely at the realities of the present moment, and in serving them experiences final reality. But he can live and fight thus with such certainty and confidence in the future because he knows that he is anchored in the mother soil of the great history of his own people and of the whole Indo-Germanic world . . .

. . . .

For us the earth is holy, because deep within it God himself dwells. According to the Christianity of the East the deeper one looks into the nature of the earthly, the more one discovers its ungodliness. Our experience is different. Wherever the searching eye and the living life is able to penetrate to the heart of things, there they encounter the God who is active and living within them. *It is for this reason* that the earth is holy for us, not because we think that it is only 'good'. This divinity is veiled in much that is mysteriously numinous, incomprehensibly awesome. We even encounter quite frequently base and questionable elements on its surface. But it is the will of God to veil himself in this way when he takes on worldly form. This in no way makes the earth any less holy for us. The distinction between holy and profane has disappeared for us. Wherever life is lived in earnest responsibility before God, everything that one does is holy . . .

And it is because the earth is so holy for us that we not only love the gifts it bestows on us with a warm love, we also steward them with deep reverence and responsibility: the bread from its soil, the waters which quench our thirst and refresh us, earthly love, the embrace of body and soul, the mother, the child which is nourished from her resources, the energy which drives us on, the battle-courage which makes us shout for joy when the moment comes to risk one's life. *Here are our sacraments, the sacraments of the earth*, which for us are more real than all others. In them the holy spirit comes upon us which surges through the world in an ever-happy Pentecost.

36 The Reich Church Committee, 15 October 1935

After the collapse of the German Christian campaign in 1933 and the failure of Müller's attempts to enforce his personal authority in 1934, the institution of a Reich Ministry of Church Affairs under Hanns Kerrl in July 1935 began the third phase in National Socialist policy towards the Protestant churches. Kerrl set up, on Reich and provincial level, Church Committees to act as an administrative umbrella beneath which the German Christians, the Confessing Church, and the 'moderates' could co-exist. Kerrl's aim was

a state church, his theology a synthesis of National Socialism and Christianity.

On the basis of the Law for the Consolidation of the German
Evangelical Church of 24 September 1935 . . . the Reich and
Prussian Minister for Church Affairs has appointed us to the
Reich Church Committee for the Evangelical Church of the Old-
Prussian Union. We have thereby taken over the duty of leading
and representing the German Evangelical Church and the Evan-
gelical Church of the Old-Prussian Union, acting as men of the
church and at the commission of the state.

We see ourselves as trustees for a transition period prior to the
emergence of an independent German Evangelical Church.

The unalterable basis of the German Evangelical Church is
the Gospel of Jesus Christ, witnessed to us in Holy Scripture and
brought to light again in the Reformation confessions (Constitution of German Evangelical Church, Article I). All the work of
the church, its theology and administration too, must serve the
proclamation of this Gospel.

Bound together by this common faith we exhort and request
the evangelical congregations to support (the people, the Reich,
and the Führer) by their intercession, loyalty, and obedience. We
affirm the National Socialist welding-together of the people on
the foundation of race, blood, and soil. We affirm the will to
freedom, national dignity, and the readiness for sacrifice, even to
the point of giving up one's life, for the sake of the German
national community.

We see in the latter the God-given reality of our German people. The church has to proclaim to this German people the Gospel of Jesus Christ . . . the saviour and redeemer of all peoples
and races. So we summon all living forces in evangelical Germany to the obedience of faith and the action of love. Above all
our desire at this present moment is to show understanding for
what, in the struggle of the past few years, have emerged so
clearly as our absolutely vital national interests and to channel
into positive commitment the energies which have been released.
This is the only way to overcome the destructive consequences
of the church conflict. . . . Tensions are unavoidable; they must
be borne with dignity, honesty, and veracity. This applies both
to us and to our opponents. So we go to work. We are conscious
of a grave and heavy responsibility, but comforted by the certainty that God can renew his church.

37 Split in the Confessing Church, October 1935

Differences as to the possibility of any cooperation with the Church Committees led to a progressive alienation between the moderate Lutherans, in the majority of the Provisional Leadership, and the radical Barmen-Dahlem group who dominated the Fraternal Council. Dr. Humburg, in his letter of 26 October 1935 to Dr. Koch, the President of the Barmen and Dahlem synods, argues that since Zoellner and the other churchmen on the Committees are state appointees to deal with them is to betray the independence of the church. To conservatives like Bishop Marahrens of Hannover this appeared an exclusivist and sectarian step into illegality.

. . . On 24 October, at 10 a.m. the local printers of Christian papers were given the following instruction by the Gestapo:

"Nothing may be printed any more in any of the church papers *against* the Church Committees; articles *supporting* the Committees may certainly be written, and edicts or statements by the Committees may be reproduced without commentary . . ." I assume that these measures have been taken without the approval of Dr. Zoellner and his colleagues. It does seem to me, however, that the Provisional Leadership of the Church must decide to break off all relations with the Committees until these measures have been withdrawn. After all, this is even worse than it was in the time of Ludwig Müller.

My view is that we cannot work together with these Committees. . . . The church can only be put in order by the church and not by the state. . . . It seems to me that our very love for our people must make us quite firm and definite in our resistance to false solutions. We must reject the claim of the state to a totality of power in relation to the church. We must help the state to find its own inner limitations . . .

The Minister for Church Affairs shares the *weltanschauung* of National Socialism. His aim is to combine this with a certain benevolence towards the church. Whether and how long this will be possible, the future will show. We certainly cannot deny him our help if, as we do not doubt, his personal intention is to do the church good. But this is precisely the reason we must tell him that this manner of proceeding is impossible. It is absolutely necessary that the church leadership which is given the task of re-ordering the church be completely free from the state and its *weltanschauung* . . .

One has to admire the persistence with which the Party and its *weltanschauung* have been directed against the church. The various attempts have really all been basically the same. The only possibility open to us is to reject any compromise, and let this principle determine our attitude to the Church Committees, too . . .

38 Censorship of the Religious Press, 15 October 1936

The ever more blatant violation of the provisions of the concordat by Party and State led to increasingly sour relations with the Roman Catholic hierarchy. Catholic organisations, schools, and newspapers were throttled out of existence by a combination of terrorism, propaganda, and 'legal' decree. Immorality trials sought to make the monastic life ridiculous. The absurd lengths to which censorship of Catholic periodicals could be taken is seen in this Reich Press Office directive.

A scrutiny of the monthly, half-monthly, and weekly editions of the *Monika* during October has revealed that despite my urgent warning of 11 May of this year you are still failing to observe the terms of my decree.

The articles 'The Dream Coffee-Warmer' and 'About Mutton' on page 10 of the monthly edition contravene the regulations. The following articles in the half-monthly and weekly edition are incompatible with the terms of my decree: 'About the Rose-Hip', 'For our Dream Living-Room', 'Everything Needed for a Baby's Doll', and 'About Nasty Creepy-Crawlies and Other Such Things'. Moreover the last-named article contains an impermissible advertisement.

The duty of a Catholic periodical, as I informed you at the time of the decree, is the nurture of religious material and ideas, every part of the contents having to deal with a religious issue.

The advertisement section of weekly edition No 40 contains the following impermissible advertisements —: Dr. Oetkers-Pudding . . .

39 Protest of the Provisional Leadership to Hitler, 28 May 1936

One of the most remarkable documents to come out of the Third Reich, this frank and brave protest, following a more specifically theological one in April 1935, goes far beyond any narrow conception of church interests. The Provisional Leadership of the Confessing Church, now in the hands of the 'radicals', raised here quite fundamental moral issues. A disastrous 'leak' of the whole document to the foreign Press gave the pretext for a wave of arrests. Possibly a rather utopian gesture at this stage, it nevertheless marked a new stage in the political awareness of German Protestantism.

. . . .

At all events, like our predecessors in office in their address of 11 April 1935 — which unfortunately has produced no visible results — we know that our sole motive for making the following statement is the duty to use our good offices on behalf of the members of the Evangelical Church in their sufferings, confusions and perils. It is our heartfelt wish that these representations will enable the Reich Government to hear with all possible clarity a voice raised out of concern for the souls entrusted to the church.
. . . .

1. *Danger of Dechristianisation*

The Provisional Leadership is well aware of the significance for 1933 and later years of the standardbearers of the National Socialist revolution being prepared to declare emphatically, "By our victory over Bolshevism we have at the same time overthrown the enemy which was attacking and threatening to destroy Christianity and the Christian churches."

Our experience, however, is that never since 1918 has the attack on the Christian church been so effectively and energetically waged as now . . .
. . . .

A responsible church leadership has the duty to resist this endangering of the members of the church. As part of this resistance it must lay before the Führer and Chancellor of the Reich the direct question whether the attempt to dechristianise the German people is to become the official policy of the Government . . .

2. *Positive Christianity*

We are confident that the Government of the Reich will heed the voice of the Evangelical Church and thus prevent the religious struggle in Germany from becoming still more acute. When the NSDAP stated in its programme that it took its stand on the basis of 'positive Christianity' it was the natural and proper conclusion of the whole Christian population that this meant that in accordance with the confessions and the preaching of the church the Christian faith would be accorded freedom and protection, indeed help and encouragement, in the Third Reich.

Later on, however, influential personalities in state and Party have come to expound the term 'positive Christianity' in an arbitrary manner. The Reich Minister for Popular Enlightenment and Propaganda, for example, interpreted positive Christianity to mean merely humanitarian activity, and on occasion combined this interpretation with an attack on the Christian churches for their allegedly meagre achievements in the realm of Christian charitable action . . . ; the Reich Leader of Ideology has proclaimed his blood mysticism to be positive Christianity and Party authorities have followed his example by spreading the slander that a Christianity which adheres to the confessions and believes in Revelation is negative. (Rosenberg: "We recognise today that the central and most important beliefs of the Roman and the Protestant Church, being negative Christianity, are not in affinity with our soul; that they stand in the way of the organic forces of the peoples of nordic-racial character, and have to make way for the latter, and allow themselves to be readusted to the values of a Germanic Christianity." Appendix 5 No. 1).

. . . .

The harm done by such utterances is all the greater, when the church is never afforded the opportunity to refute before equally large audiences the false interpretations of the Christian faith propagated by these prominent public figures.

3. *Destruction of Church Order*

. . . .

There is, it is true, an official denial of any intention to encroach upon the inner structure and spiritual life of the Evangelical church. In fact, however, one encroachment has followed another since the elections forced on the church in July 1933:

A. Relating to the Church as a Whole:

1. Installation of the State Commissar in Prussia on 24 June, 1933, and of State Commissars in Bremen, Hesse, Lippe, Mecklenburg, Saxony.

2. Promulgation of general Church elections by Reich Law of 15 July, 1933.

3. Radio speech by the Führer of 22 July, 1933, in favour of the German Christians.
4. Prohibition of publications about Church matters by the unpublished order of the Reich Minister of the Interior on 6 and 7 November, 1934.
5. Establishment of the State Finance Department by the Prussian Law of March 1935.
6. Establishment of the Decision Centre by the Reich Law of June 1935.
7. Law for the Consolidation of the German Evangelical Church of 24 September 1935, and the Church Committees set up thereafter.
B. Relating to Individual Clergy:
1. Arrest of bishops of Württemberg and Bavaria, 1934.
2. Despatch of clergy to concentration camps, especially in Saxony and Nassau-Hesse.
3. Expulsion of clergy from their parish area, or even from their home province, especially in Prussia.
4. Arrest of 700 pastors in Prussia as a result of the pulpit declaration against Neopaganism ordered by the Old Prussian Synod in March 1935.
5. Obstruction of special Confessing Church Services . . . (Appendix 7).

. . . The so-called 'Pacification Action', initiated with the establishment of the Reich Ministry for Church Affairs and the installation of the Church Committees, may have put an end to some of the abuses hitherto perpetrated by state officials or Party members and tolerated by the state. However, the Evangelical Christian who takes a closer look will realise that the effect of this 'Pacification Action' is to bring the church into financial and organisational dependence upon the state, to rob her of the freedom of her preaching and church order, and to compel her to tolerate false teaching . . .

4. *Deconfessionalisation*

Under the slogans of 'deconfessionalisation' or 'transcending the confessional division' a movement has developed with the aim of making the wider outreach of the church impossible. For a long time now the Evangelical Church has been deprived of its own youth organisations. . . . The top leadership of organised youth movements has consistently sought to impress upon even the smallest groupings of Evangelical youth the view that their church is contemptible and suspect . . . (— Where are the enemies of our Hitler Youth? The religious fanatic, who even in our day drops to his knees with his eyes fixed longingly upwards, who spends his time on church services and prayers. . . . As

Hitler boys we can have only contempt or disdain for those young people who even in our day still run to their ridiculous Evangelical or Catholic clubs, in order to devote themselves to completely superfluous religious sentimentalism — Appendix 9, Nr. I).

Although the present state officially supports positive Christianity its new institutions such as the *Year on the Land* or the *Labour Service* offer almost no possibilities of pastoral care for their members . . .

The deconfessionalisation of the school is deliberately furthered by the state. The abolition of the confessional school is pushed forward in violation of the church's rights, and in the process the consciences of the parents come under the strongest pressure from the Party. The legitimate curricula for religious instruction are frequently neglected, with the result that in many places essential elements of biblical material are already being eliminated from religious instruction (Old Testament) or un-Christian material inserted (Old-German Paganism). School services and church parades are being increasingly neglected . . .

At the universities the training of theological students is being entrusted more and more to professors and lecturers who are proven teachers of false doctrine . . .

The 'deconfessionalisation of *public* life' also amounts to dechristianisation, for Christian influence and Christian participation in radio, Press, and in public lectures are being pushed more and more into the background.

5. *National Socialist Weltanschauung*

Evangelical members of the NS organisations are compelled to give their unconditional allegiance to the National Socialist *weltanschauung*. . . . If this means that blood, race, nationality, and honour are to be regarded as eternal values, the First Commandment constrains the Evangelical Christian to reject this evaluation. Where Aryan man is glorified, God's Word witnesses to the fallenness of all men; where anti-semitism is forced on the Christian in the context of the National Socialist *weltanschauung*, obligating him to *hate* the Jews, the Christian command to love one's neighbour points in the opposite direction.

6. *Morality and Justice*

We note with grave concern that a totally alien morality to that of Christianity is permeating our people and threatening to undermine it. . . . The good is now generally defined as that which furthers the interests of the people.

. . . .

Evangelical Christians are convinced on the basis of Holy

61

Scripture that God is the protector of justice and of those to whom justice is denied; hence they regard it as apostasy from Him when arbitrariness finds its way into judicial matters and things happen, "which are not just in the sight of the Lord." Not only are many incidents during the Church Struggle of relevance here, but also the virtual withdrawal of legal protection by the institution and administration of the Church 'Decision Centre' . . . . The Evangelical conscience, aware of its co-responsibility for people and Government, is most severely burdened by the fact that in Germany, which describes itself as a state where law prevails, concentration camps still exist, and that the measures of the state secret police are still exempt from any judicial investigation. . .

7. *The Claim of God*

We request the Government of the Reich to ask itself whether in the long run it can benefit our nation if the course taken thus far is proceeded with in the future. Already the violation of conscience, the persecution of evangelical convictions, the mutual spying and eavesdropping exercise a disastrous influence. Even an exalted cause must in the end lead the nation to ruin if it sets itself against the revealed will of God. God's church will endure, even if in the attempt to dechristianise the German people millions of Evangelical Christians must forfeit their salvation . . .

Our people threatens to transgress the limits set it by God. It seeks to make itself the measure of all things. That is human arrogance, setting itself up against God.

. . . A few years ago the Führer still disapproved of the placing of his picture on evangelical altars. Today his views are made in a more and more extreme manner the norm not only of political decisions but also of morality and justice in our people, and he himself is invested with the religious status of the people's priest, indeed of the mediator between God and people.

What we have said in this address to the Führer the stewardship of our office compelled us to say. The Church stands in the hand of her Lord . . .

40 Seamen's Mission Library, 16 July 1936

The detailed surveillance of church institutions, carried out partly by Kerrl's Ministry for Church Affairs, is illustrated by this report. Many, though not all, of the books are by National Socialist or kindred authors.

Surveillance of Church Life

16 July 1936

Apostolate of the Ocean
German Catholic Seamen's Mission
Central Office Bremerhaven

To His Excellency
The Reich Minister for Church Affairs

. . . In reference to your enquiry about the promotion of National Socialist writings and books among the seamen under our care we would respectfully draw your attention to the enclosed list of the books which we have in stock. At the same time we can inform you that our homes display not only the *Völkischer Beobachter* but also the *Illustrierter Beobachter* on their literature racks . . .

List of the history books held in the library of the Catholic Seamen's Mission, Bremerhaven:

G	1	*Deutsche Geschichte*	Pinnow
	2	*Deutsche Geschichte*	Nobel
	3	*Die Amerikaner*	Münsterberg
	4	*Abrüstung oder Kriegsvorbereitungen*	Oertzen
	5	*Deutschlands blutende Grenze*	Martel
	6	*Deutschland und England*	Sieper
	7	*Der Geist der Paulskirche*	Petzel
	8	*Gespenster am Toten Mann*	Ettinghofer
	9	*Enthüllungen*	Deltour
	10	*Deutschland im Weltkrieg*	Landmann
	11	*Die russische Gottlosenbewegung*	Ziegler
	12	*Der Bolschewismus*	Gurian
	13	*Das dritte Reich*	van den Brück
	14	*Mein Kampf*	Hitler
	15	*Sozialismus und Aussenpolitik*	van den Brück
	16	*Vom Kaiserhof zur Reichskanzlei*	Dr. Goebbels
	17	*Hitlers Wollen*	Siebarth
	18	*Wir bauen das Dritte Reich*	Dr. Frich
	19	*Politische Jugend*	Rau
	20	*Der Weg des politischen Katholizismus in Deutschland*	Ritter
	20ª	*Reden aus Kampf und Sieg*	Goebbels-Beumelburg

21 *Reden zur nationalen Revolution*   Papen
22 *Die Revolution ist nicht das*
   Ende   Spengler
23 *Der Glaube an Deutschland*   Zöberlein
24 *Hitlers Kampf für den Frieden*   Hadamowsky

41 Agreement between the Reich Church Committee and the Leaders of the Provincial Churches, 20 November 1936

Signed, among others, by Bishops Marahrens, Wurm, and Meiser (of Hannover, Württemberg, and Bavaria), this advocacy of Church Committees for the 'non-intact churches' was regarded as a betrayal of the ideals of Barmen and Dahlem by the radical wing of the Confessing Church. The Lutherans had already suspended all relations with the Provisional Leadership following the publication of the protest to Hitler (nr. 39). As a strong, united force the Confessing Church was at an end.

. . . It is imperative that the Reich Church Committee be given the opportunity to initiate and bring to a successful conclusion all measures which will further the reconstruction and the work of the church. Above all, the measures for restoring order, based on the Law for the Consolidation of the German Evangelical Church of 24 September 1935, . . . should be implemented without delay in those provincial churches in which order has not yet been restored.
. . . .
We, together with the Reich Church Committee, stand behind the Führer in the life-struggle of the German people against Bolshevism. For this struggle the church mobilises the forces of Christian belief against unbelief, Christian morality against amorality, the obedient submission to God's will as Creator

64

against the loosing of all organic ties. We will be untiring in
calling upon our congregations to commit all Christian forces to
this struggle, knowing that this will be rendering the German
people a most valuable service.

We expect, however, a complete cessation to the anti-
Christian propaganda which has emerged of late more and more
unashamedly in periodicals, newspapers, and training courses,
and in innumerable statements even by leading officials . . .

. . . .

42 Hitler Announces New Church Elections, 15 February 1937

In fact the elections intimated here never took place, due
to the turmoil being created by Kerrl. In a last attempt to
enforce his concept of a state church some seven hundred
pastors, including Martin Niemöller himself, were arrested.
Niemöller's dramatic acquittal, in a blaze of international
publicity, did not prevent him being consigned to a concentration camp, where he was to remain until the end of the
Third Reich. Meanwhile the SS solution of a complete separation of church and state gained increasing favour in Party
circles.

Now that the Reich Church Committee has failed to bring
about a unification of the church groups of the German Evangelical Church the church, acting in complete freedom as the
church people themselves decide, will give itself the new constitution and thereby a new order. I therefore empower the Reich
Minister for Church Affairs to arrange the election of a General
Synod for this purpose and to take such measures as are necessary for this.

43 The Jewishness of Christianity, End February 1938

Dibelius, preacher at the pompous inauguration of the
Hitler régime at Potsdam, had defended the boycott of Jew-

ish businesses in a 1933 broadcast to America. By 1937 the conduct of Müller and Kerrl had made him a firm defender of the independence of the church and had sharpened his awareness of the Jewish roots of Christianity. The result of this letter to Kerrl was a show trial at which he was acquitted. The reference to Bishop Galen shows how the Protestant and Catholic churches were beginning, belatedly, to recognise their common interests.

Most honoured Herr Reich Minister,

On 13 February you addressed the presidents of the Church Committees you instituted. Now speeding through the Evangelical Church of Germany, this address has approximately the same significance for the relationship between the Evangelical Church and your Ministry as the Sports Palace meeting of November 1933 had for the relationship between us and the German Christians; the veil is fallen which up to now hid the reality from many eyes; the opposing standpoints are clear; it is now obvious to everyone what the Church Ministry has been seeking to achieve by its measures hitherto and what it seeks to achieve for the future.
. . . .

Your address was meant to explain the new organisational form for the Evangelical Church. The decision of the Führer has set this organisational form aside. This, however, only disposes of one part of your speech. There remains the other, in which you have expounded the principles which you believe should determine your actions as Minister of Church Affairs.

According to the report before me you said: The Catholic bishop Graf Galen and the Evangelical General-Superintendent Zoellner had sought to instruct you about the nature of Christianity — namely that it was a matter of recognising that Jesus was God's Son. That was ridiculous and of peripheral importance. To let the person of Jesus influence one and to live out a practical Christianity — that was everything. The Apostle's Creed had been put together during the church's history. It was nonsense to make the recognition of this Apostle's Creed a mark of true Christianity. Pfleiderer has said: God reveals himself in history; dogmas are the work of men.

. . . But if Jesus of Nazareth was a man like the rest of us then anyone can criticise and alter his teaching. Then the sacraments of the church no longer have any meaning. Then the church has no longer the right to set against the *Myth* of Alfred Rosenberg the Gospel as the eternal, unchangeable truth of God . . .

You have gone still further. You have insisted that the preaching of the Evangelical Church should change. . . . You have said: The will of the Father, which according to the words of Jesus we should fulfil, is given us in our blood.

The New Testament knows nothing about the will of God being given us in our blood . . .

You have also said: The priests declare that Jesus was a Jew; they spoke of the Jew Paul and stated that salvation came from the Jews. This was quite unacceptable.

I cannot recall that the preaching of the Evangelical Church has previously given any particular emphasis to these matters. However now that the attacks of the opponents make a point of concentrating on this point the church is certainly obliged to say: Yes, indeed, Jesus of Nazareth, as far as his human nature is concerned, is of the family of David and therefore a Jew! The New Testament teaches this clearly and unmistakeably. . . . If you say that it is impossible for evangelical pastors to say these things then this means that you want to prevent the pastors saying what is in the New Testament . . .

. . . If that is not an encroachment on the proclamation of the church I do not know what on earth can be understood as an encroachment on the proclamation of the church. Here is the point where the church must resist and will resist . . .

. . . .

Here is the decisive point. If you demand that the Evangelical Church should not be a state within the state every evangelical Christian will say 'Yes' to that. Church should be church, not a state within the state. However, the principles you enunciate amount to this: that the state should become church, by legislating about preaching and about the faith which men should confess, and by using the forcible means at its disposal to support such legislation. Here lies the root of the whole struggle between the state and the Evangelical Church . . .

. . . .

44 "With Burning Concern", 14 March 1937

This encyclical of Pius XI, addressed to the German episcopate and read out from every Catholic pulpit on 21 March 1937, provoked a furious reaction from the

NSDAP and undoubtedly represented a hardening of the papal line, which lasted until Pacelli became Pius XII two years later. Hitherto protests had been confidential and through the normal diplomatic channels. Now the breakdown of the concordat and the conflict between the claims of National Socialism and Christianity is publicly acknowledged. The language, however, especially on the larger moral issues, is very vague.

With burning concern and mounting consternation we have been observing for some time now the cross carried by the church in Germany and the increasingly difficult situation of those men and women who have kept the faith and remained true to her in thought and deed — all this in the midst of the land and the people to which St. Boniface once brought the Gospel of Light, the glad tidings of Christ and the Kingdom of God.
. . . .
When We, reverend brethren, accepted the proposal of the Reich Government in the summer of 1933 to engage in negotiations about a concordat on the basis of a draft dating back several years, these negotiations ending, to the satisfaction of all of you, with a solemn agreement. We were motivated by dutiful concern for the freedom of the saving mission of the church in Germany and for the salvation of the souls entrusted to her — but at the same time We also genuinely wished to make a significant contribution to the peaceful development and welfare of the German people.

Hence despite some grave misgivings We made the agonising decision not to withhold Our assent. As far as humanly possible We wanted to spare our loyal sons and daughters in Germany the tensions and sufferings which would certainly have been expected otherwise under the circumstances of the time . . .

If the tree of peace which We have planted in German soil has not borne the fruit which, with the interests of your people in mind, We had hoped for, no one in the whole wide world, who has eyes to see and ears to hear, will still be able to say today that the blame for this lies on the side of the church and of its head. The past years make it all too clear where the responsibility lies. They unveil conspiracies which from the very beginning envisaged nothing else than a battle to the death . . .

. . . When the time comes to set before the eyes of the world what We have tried to do it will be clear to all men of good will where the conservers and where the disrupters of the peace are to be sought. Anyone who still has within him the slightest feeling for truth, whose heart has even a shadowy sense of justice will have to admit then that in these difficult and eventful years which have followed the Concordat every one of Our words and every one of Our deeds have been regulated by loyalty to the agreement which was made. He will, however, also have to note with consternation and the deepest disapproval how for the other side it has become the unwritten law of their conduct to misconstrue, evade, undermine, and in the end more or less openly violate the treaty.

That We, despite all, continued to display moderation was due not to wordly considerations of expediency and still less to unbecoming weakness but purely because of the desire not to pull out good growth together with the tares; because of Our intention not to make any public pronouncement until men's minds were ready to recognise the inevitability of such a pronouncement . . .

. . . .

Above all, take care, reverend brethren, that the belief in God, the primary and irreplaceable basis of all religion, remains pure and uncorrupted in German territories. The oratorical use of the word God does not make someone a believer in God, only the use of this august word within the framework of a true and worthy concept of God.

. . . .

Race, nation, state, the form of the state, the holding of office within the state, and other such basic constituents of human society all have an essential and honourable place within the secular order. To abstract them, however, from the earthly scale of values and make them the supreme norm of all values, including religious ones, and divinize them with an idolatrous cult, is to be guilty of perverting and falsifying the order of things created and commanded by God . . .

. . . .

God has given his commandments in sovereign form. Their validity transcends time and space, country and race. . . . The totality of his rights as Creator legitimates, in accordance with his nature, the totality of his claim on the obedience of the individual and on the various forms of communal life. This claim to obedience embraces all realms of life in which moral questions require recourse to the divine law, so that transient human judgment can be set within the framework of the unchangeable divine judgment.

. . . .

The culmination of Revelation in the Gospel of Jesus Christ is final, is binding for ever. This Revelation has no room for addenda made by human hand, still less for an ersatz or substitute religion based on arbitrary *revelations*, which some contemporary advocates wish to derive from the so-called myth of blood and race . . .

. . . .

In your areas, reverend brethren, the choir of voices calling for people to leave the church is becoming louder and louder. Not infrequently among the advocates of this course of action are those who use their official position to create the impression that to leave the church and thus display disloyalty to Christ the King is a particularly convincing and meritorious way of demonstrating one's loyalty to the present state . . .

Faith in the church will not be maintained pure and unsullied unless it is supported by faith in the primacy of the bishop of Rome. . . . If people, who are not even one in Christ, seek to entice you with the utopia of a German national church, note this well: it is nothing but a denial of the one church of Christ, a blatant departure from the missionary mandate to the whole world; only a universal church can carry this out properly . . .

. . . .

Human laws which are irreconcilable with natural law, are born with a defect that no forcible constraints, no outward display of power can remedy. The principle 'Whatever benefits the people is just' must also be judged in this light . . .

. . . .

Conscientious parents, aware of their educational duties, have a primal and original right to determine that the children which God has given them should be educated in the spirit of the true faith and in accordance with its principles and instructions . . .

The church, therefore, which is called upon to protect and expound the divine law of nature, has no option but to pronounce the recent school enrolments, which took place with a notorious lack of freedom, as products of compulsion and as devoid of all legal validity.

. . . .

No one has the slightest intention of putting any obstacles in the way of the pursuit by the youth of Germany of the realisation of true national community, of the nurture of the noble love of freedom, of inviolable loyalty to the fatherland. What We do oppose and what We must oppose is the deliberate and carefully fostered contradiction which is being opened up between these educational objectives and religious ones. . . . He who sings the song of allegiance to his earthly fatherland, must not become a deserter and traitor by disloyalty to his God, his church, and his eternal fatherland . . .

. . . .

45 Kassel Statement to Congregations, 29 August 1937

The contorted thinking and ambiguous wording of this protest reflect the tensions within the 'Kassel Executive' itself: Marahrens, F. Müller (of the Provisional Leadership), and Breit (of the Lutheran Council). It was founded in an attempt to patch up the disputes between the various groupings in the Confessing Church, as Kerrl's campaign of persecution reached its height.

The distress caused by the grave struggles now in progress brought together representatives from almost all the German provincial churches at Kassel on 5 and 16 July 1937. They despatched a joint memorandum to the Reich Government requesting a personal audience, since the policies pursued at the moment by the state cannot lead to a pacification of the churches; on the contrary they consistently accentuate the differences . . .

I

Our politically unified nation is being confronted as a result of these religious controversies with decisions which can shake it to its very foundations. It is the distress of the present time, but also its dignity, that there is no way of evading these life and death questions for our nation; they must be faced . . .

It is quite self-evident that more and more it is the question of questions which is being raised, the question of faith, the question about God. The passionately and forcefully presented claims of nation and state confront the claims of God to which the Christian church is called to witness. After a difficult period of decay and disintegration which led us close to the brink of the

71

death of our nation our people and our state can only be healed and strengthened if every member of the nation is challenged and grasped to the very depths of his being. The Christian faith in God, however, proclaims the Gospel of the God who claims the whole of man as his own. Our nation must find a solution to the question of how the claim of the state and the claim of the living God stand in relation to one another. What better way of achieving this than that of struggle and suffering? The gravity of the decisions which are expected of us here promises rich fruit and blessing. Thus this struggle, which is anything but an idle quarrel, is genuinely about the Faith itself and therefore about the future of our German people.

. . . .

46 The SS and the Jesuits, August 1937

Himmler had an almost neurotic regard for the Society of Jesus, and consciously sought to incorporate some of its élitist features in the SS, while regarding it as one of National Socialism's most formidable enemies. This extract comes from an SS instruction manual about the Jesuits, issued in August 1937.

Summary:

As the fighting corps of the Vatican, the Jesuit order, with its multifarious contacts, the outstanding training of its members, and its brilliant operational methods, is one of the most important instruments of the Church's power politics.

This body of men, organised along strictly hierarchical lines, combines the tasks of defence against opponents, positive attack on the enemy and the gathering of information for the Vatican.

Its great successes in gathering information, which above all else maintains the regard in which the Jesuit order is held at the Vatican, are due mainly to the fact that to the onlooker the work of gathering information appears quite secondary to the role assigned it in the ideological struggle. By means of the ideological struggle and the specialist knowledge of the Society of Jesus which subserves it the Jesuits have created such a widespread net of contacts that sources of information are automatically available to them.

On the other hand their brilliant information service enables the Jesuits to know before anyone else where attacks or counter-measures are to be expected and hence they are also in the best position for a successful conduct of the Church's attacks and counter-measures.

For almost four hundred years this method of combining an information service with a troop to defend and propagate its ideology has been successfully tested by the Jesuits.

47 **The Werner Era Begins, 10 December 1937**

This decree by Kerrl effectively put the control of the German Evangelical Church in the hands of Dr. Werner, a German Christian. His Chancellery grew in importance as the Ministry of Church Affairs lost Party support. By a network of bureaucratic controls, legal and financial, it conducted a fairly successful war of attrition against the Confessing Church. The work of the Provisional Leadership, above all the training of its future clergy, could now only continue illegally.

1

1. The leadership of the German Evangelical Church is in the hands of the Director of the German Evangelical Church Chancellery.
2. The latter is empowered, after consultation with the church governments of the provincial churches, to issue decrees on matters of externals. Questions relating to confession and worship are excluded from this authorisation.

3

1. The leadership of the church designated by this decree means primarily the exercise of the right to govern the church including the issuing of decrees.

48 Report on Beuron Monastery, 20 April 1938

This is one of several reports on the political reliability of the Benedictine arch-abbey of Beuron by Dr. Simons, the Provincial Governor of the Hohenzollern territories, to the Ministry for Church Affairs. Dated 20 April 1938, this report welcomes the change in political alignments which has followed the replacement of Dr. Raphael Walzer, the previous arch-abbot, by Dr. Benedict Baur.

In the plebiscite on 10 April [to approve the annexation of Austria] those belonging to the monastery voted 'Yes' almost without exception. Or the evening of 12 April, when the evening meal was over, the arch-abbot held an address — normally not a word is spoken in the refectory — in which he made reference to the results of the plebiscite. Of 417 entitled to vote . . . 408 voted 'Yes' and 9 'No'. . . . The arch-abbot explained that he could not understand how there could still be 9 people in Beuron entitled to vote who had wanted to withhold their approval from the Führer; after all he had safeguarded us from bolshevistic chaos and brought Germany political and economic success . . .

49 The Silencing of the Churches, 12 September 1938

What at first sight might appear to be a rather schizophrenic attitude to the Churches on the part of National Socialism was in fact dictated by the need to retain the allegiance of the millions of largely nominal Christians of the older generation, while providing new patterns of allegiance for the new political élite and for the coming generation. Hess's speech to the Gauleiters at Nuremberg on 12 September 1938 is one of the clearest expositions of this policy, which involved the 'deconfessionalisation' of public life, and the quiet promotion of the Party as the eventual successor to the Churches.

The decision of the Party not to become involved in the Church Struggle has proved to be a completely correct one. It was right that local leaders were forbidden to urge people to leave the Church or to prevent Party comrades entering churches, celebrating church marriages, baptisms, etc.

A religion which has influenced, indeed at times even dominated, the whole life of the nation for two millennia, cannot be destroyed or overcome by external pressures — and certainly not by any crude story-telling, mockery, or denying of the Godhead such as may have taken place. Lack of tact or good taste in this realm can all too easily repel men who otherwise are enthusiastic supporters of the new Reich and drive them into the ranks of the silent Opposition, even in political matters. This cannot be said too often.

Moreover such methods are more likely to create 'church-goers', than men with a new experience of faith.

The more we National Socialists avoid religious controversies, abstain from Church ceremonies, but on the other hand win the confidence of the people by our dutifulness, justice, and loyalty, the more men will feel that they belong to National Socialism. The more National Socialism is seen as a blessing as a result of our work and the conviction spreads that Providence is with us and with our work, the more people will recognise that National Socialism is a God-ordained order and institution. Thus they will gradually become increasingly alienated by the Churches and their dogmas in the degree to which the latter stand in our way.

For the rest, the tactic of condemning them to silence has been completely successful. Who bothers any longer if, for example, pastoral letters are read from the pulpits of the Catholic churches — however packed they may be with concealed threats, attacks, distortions of the truth, and so on . . . ? Their lordships can read out what they want as long as they have no access to the outside world. They will not tempt us to retort with the counter-propaganda they would like to see . . .

The Church question remains for the foreseeable future a question of the attitudes of the coming generation. These attitudes, however, are formed not only by the training of the HJ [Hitler Youth]. The parental home still plays a part. The less parents are antagonised, especially in Church matters, the less they will be inclined to vent their ill-will by undermining the influence of the HJ.

50 The Munich Crisis, 19 September 1938

The churches' growing alarm at the 'cultural' policies of the Third Reich did not imply any disapproval of its foreign policy: the exit from the League of Nations, rearmament, the incorporation of the Saar and of Austria, the demand for the surrender of the Sudetenland. Hence Karl Barth's letter to Professor Hromadka, written on the eve of Munich, met with almost total astonishment and repudiation. Even the Provisional Leadership of the Confessing Church distanced itself from it. Barth, dismissed from his Bonn chair in 1934, had since then been teaching in Basel, and his influence on the Confessing Church was now a limited one.

. . . Has the whole world, then, fallen under the spell of the evil eye of Leviathan? And must the pacifism of the post-war era really lead to such a terrible paralysis of decision on the part of each and every power today? And worst of all: although the Western Powers do not seem as yet to have bowed to the senseless demands of Germany, what will happen if they do so after all? Will your Government and your people remain firm despite this, indeed all the more determinedly? I can well foresee what an infinite burden of distress you would thereby bring upon yourselves. Yet I dare to hope that the sons of the old Hussites will then show a Europe which has gone too soft that there are still men alive today. Every Czech soldier who fights and suffers will then do it on our behalf as well — and, I say it without qualification, will also do it on behalf of the church of Jesus Christ which faces nothing but ridicule or extinction in the atmosphere of Hitler and Mussolini.

I still cannot suppress the hope that if Prague remains firm London and Paris will perhaps become firm again. One certainly cannot contemplate the possibility of Russian assistance with any pleasure, because even if it were effective it would mean the driving out of the devil by Beelzebub. But what, in the last resort, do we know of the plans and intentions of the providence of God which may be being accomplished through all this?

. . . .

51 The Intercession Liturgy, 27 September 1938

Another reaction to the Munich crisis was the production by the Provisional Leadership of this liturgy. Its measured sobriety and concern for peace were stamped by a hysterically militaristic Press as a defeatist erosion of national morale. Its authors, branded as 'traitors', had their pay blocked, and further disciplinary measures threatened. The bishops of the 'intact churches' of Hannover, Württemberg, Bavaria, and Baden also condemned the liturgy which, since the Munich Agreement removed for the moment the danger of war, was never actually used.

1. Hymn 140: In deep distress . . .
2. My friends, in the great troubles which have befallen us, let us turn our hearts to God, who is our confidence and our strength, to hear his Word and to offer Him our prayers. Hear then the Word of God, as it is written in Psalm 32:

    Happy the man to whom the Lord does not attribute evil, in whose spirit there is no falsehood . . .
3. Prayer: Let us confess our sin to God and seek forgiveness for the sake of our Lord Jesus Christ:

    Lord our God, we poor sinners confess before you the sin of our church, of its leaders, congregations, and pastors. Often we have hindered the spread of your Word by lovelessness, often we have destroyed the credibility of your Word by our fear of men. All too often we have shown tolerance to a false Gospel. Our lives have not been such that men could see our good works and praise you. We confess before you the sins of our nation. Within it your name has often been blasphemed, your Word attacked, your truth suppressed. In public and in secret much injustice has been committed. Parents and masters are despised, lives harmed and destroyed, marriage broken, property stolen, and the honour of one's neighbour impugned. Lord, our God, we lay before you in penitence these sins of ours and these sins of our people. Forgive us and temper justice with mercy. Amen.

4. Hymn 34: O Lamb of God
5. Scripture Reading . . .
6. Prayer: Let us then beseech God of his grace to keep war from us and our land and to grant peace to us and our children.
   Period of quiet
   Lord, Our God, turn away war from us! Guide the hearts of those who bear authority in all countries. O God, may they lead their nations in the way of peace! Amen.

. . . .

8. If, however, God in his unsearchable wisdom punishes us with war, let us find comfort in his promise. Hear God's Word, as it is written in Psalm 91:
   He who sits in the protection of the Most High and abides under the shadow of the Almighty . . .
9. Prayer: We remember before God all those who are called to arms. May God strengthen them when they have to leave home and hearth, wife and child, when they suffer all manner of privations in the face of the foe, when they are wounded or fall ill, when they are captured or snatched away by death.

. . . .

12. Prayer: We remember the mothers who fear for their sons, the women who wait for the return of their husbands, the children whose father is absent. We intercede for the men and women employed in the war industries, for all who have to provide the nation with its daily bread, and also for all those who are alone, whose fate will be forgotten;

. . . .

15. Prayer: We remember before God the young and the old who will be torn away from their ordered way of life. We think of the lonely men and women, the unprotected boys and girls. We remember all those who may be tempted to exercise frightful vengeance and to be overcome by hate. We remember the men whose country is threatened by war and pray to God for them all.

. . . .

17. At times such as these God the Lord has assigned the church special tasks. Woe to any nation in which the church does not carry out its task at this time . . .
18. Prayer: We remember the holy Christian church in all nations. We pray for its elders and pastors who have to speak the Gospel without fear today as everyday. We pray for those in leadership in the church who have to watch lest the

truth of the Word of God be corrupted. We pray for the congregations, that they will remain firm in the fellowship of the Word of God. We pray for all who suffer persecution for Christ's sake.

. . . .

52 Foreign Policy and the Churches, 1938

This brief extract from the 1938 report of the RHSA (Central Office for Reich Security) highlights the violent anti-clericalism of the SS rather than giving an objective picture of Church attitudes which were, on the whole, conventionally patriotic. These reports do, however, provide a useful corrective to any tendency to regard the Churches as playing a mere 'fellow-traveller' role.

Political Churches

. . . Up to the middle of the summer of 1938 the position of the Churches was characterised by weariness, uncertainty, depression.

The situation altered, however, overnight at the end of August when the foreign situation became increasingly acute. Church forces at once saw in the foreign affairs crisis the possibility that National Socialist power could collapse. They hoped in turn that a collapse of this nature would lead to a revival of their ecclesiastical power. With services of intercession, prophecies of an imminent war and the coming collapse of the Third Reich, with references to the defeat in the World War, with a campaign to spread rumours and unrest, Church groupings of the most varied kind attempted to infect the people as a whole with uncertainty and nervousness and thereby to weaken the impact of the Third Reich in foreign affairs. During this crisis period in international politics the treacherous activities and attitudes of the Church groupings within Germany was allied with the universalist propaganda of World Catholicism, World Protestantism and the internationalist sects.

Hence the Munich Agreement and the peaceable settlement of the conflict was no small surprise for the Churches. They soon found a way out of their confusion, however, by characterising the Munich Agreement as being primarily due to the prayers of the priests and the faithful and as a wondrous intervention of God and St. Michael, on whose feast the Munich Agreement was signed. The leaders of the Churches did, however, decide to retire somewhat from the public eye for a while.

. . . .

Yet even after the return of the East March [Austria] to the Reich the German bishops kept up their stubborn resistance. Bishop Preysing at once saw to the prohibition of all propaganda for the referendum in the Church Press and to a ban on all pulpit announcements affirming state and nation in order to sabotage as effectively as possible the national referendum of 10/4/38.

. . . .

53 Theology Faculties in the Universities, 21 February 1939

In close cooperation with the SS and NSDAP headquarters the Ministry of Education drew up various plans for the gradual phasing out of the theological faculties, Catholic and Protestant. The seminaries of the Confessing Church had already been declared illegal in 1937. The outbreak of the War delayed somewhat the realisation of these ideas. By 1939 only 2% of university students read theology, compared with 6% in 1933. This memorandum from Heydrich was regarded by the Ministry as much too cautious.

The Catholic University System for Training Candidates for the Priesthood.

. . . .

It must be the long-term aim of the National Socialist state to carry out rigorously the separation of church and state, thus leaving the training of her clergy to the church itself and stage by stage dismantling the still existent apparatus of state theological faculties and state colleges of philosophy and theology.

. . . .

By carrying out a stage by stage reduction of the theological faculties and the colleges of philosophy and theology to the minimum number of chairs required by church regulations these state institutions will speedily decline into insignificance. It is to be expected that the church will exercise its right, conceded in the Concordat, to set up its own seminaries for ordinands. This would leave the way open for the complete elimination of state institutions for the training of priests.

. . . .

54 Research Institute into Jewish Influence on German Church Life, 6 May 1939

The persecution of the Confessing Church, the timidity of the Lutheran leaders, and the sponsorship of Werner all encouraged a certain recovery in German Christian fortunes. In April 1939 there had appeared the notorious Godesberg Declaration, to which—ominously—the prestigious Bishop Marahrens had lent his signature. Even in the modified form acceptable to the other leaders of the 'intact' churches it affirmed the necessity of an "earnest, responsible racial policy to keep our nation pure." On the heels of this came the opening on 6 May of the research institute advertised here with its avowed aim of 'dejudaizing' the church.

The foundation of this institute is based on the conviction that Jewish influence on all areas of German life, including therefore that of religion and of the church, must be brought to light and eliminated.

Christianity has nothing in common with Judaism. From the *Gospel of Christ* on it has developed in *opposition to Judaism* and has always been attacked by the latter. Its eternal truth has been of decisive importance in our people's history by welding Germany into one. The eternal power of this truth means that particularly in the Germany of our own day Christianity has the task of promoting a true renewal of genuine religious life in our nation. Since alien Jewish influences have gained foot within Christianity itself over the course of its historical development, the *Dejudaisation of the Church and of Christianity* has become

81

the inescapable and decisive task for contemporary church life; *it is the presupposition for the future of Christianity.*

With this aim in mind the task of the institute is to make an exact and detailed investigation into the manner and degree of Jewish influence on church life by thorough scholarly research. Leading scholars and churchmen will work together side by side in their determination to carry out this task.

On the basis of the results of this scholarly research it will then be possible to rid the church life of the German people of those elements which derive from Jewish influence and to clear the way for a faith springing from the unadulterated Gospel of Christ to place itself at the disposal of the German people for the creation of its religious community.

. . . .

55 The Jewish Christian

Even in its shattered condition during the War the Confessing Church showed an unusual measure of concern for its Jewish Christian members. The first extract is taken from a letter sent by Pastor Müller, the chairman of the Provisional Leadership, to the German-Christian President of the Supreme Church Council, Dr. Werner, on 4 November 1939; the second, dated September 1942, from a statement issued by the Confessing Synod of the Brandenburg province.

(a)

Some months ago the Consistories sent out questionnaires to the pastors requesting them to give information about their Aryan heredity. Pastors who refused to give information of this nature are still being pressed to do so by the Church authorities . . .

We would recall that the illegitimate synod of September 1933 saw the first attempt to introduce the Aryan paragraph into the Church and that this attempt failed due to the united stand of the holders of spiritual office.

. . . .

Today the Evangelical Supreme Church Council and the Consistories are again taking up this important issue. But no mention is being made of it to the Church at large; on the contrary, it is intended, if possible, to implement it in complete secrecy. No decree has been issued relating to the introduction of the Aryan paragraph into the Church. . . . What cannot be achieved in an ecclesiastically legitimate manner, since there is no doubt that it is contrary to Holy Scripture, is to be implemented by administrative means . . .

. . . .

That a total perversion of the nature of the spiritual office is intended is quite clear from a decree of the Supreme Church Council of 12/5/39, which makes the presentation of evidence of Aryan descent a condition for admission to a theological examination or ordination or for an appointment with tenure to a parish church . . .

We are constrained to inform the Supreme Church Council that pastors may not cooperate with this attempt to convert the office of preaching into an institution determined by political principles, in this case principles at complete variance with those recognised by the Church . . .

(b)

The exclusion of non-Aryan Christians from the fellowship of the Church is contrary to the nature of the sacrament of Holy Baptism, contrary to the statements of Holy Scripture in Romans XI about Israel according to the flesh, contrary to the fellowship and unity of all Christians witnessed to by the apostle Paul in Galatians 3^{28} and contrary to the third article of the Confession of Faith.

. . . .

The exclusion of non-Aryan Christians from the fellowship of the Church is contrary to Holy Scripture and to the Confession of the Church and is therefore invalid by Church law. We exhort pastors and congregations in the name of Christ to maintain church fellowship with them.

56 The Outbreak of War, 2 September 1939

The three man Advisory Council which issued this statement was appointed by Werner on 31 August 1939, its most prominent member being Bishop Marahrens. Neither Catholic nor Protestant churchmen felt any hesitations about lending the war their moral support, the only options—pacifism or resistance—being equally unthinkable. The exaggerated servility of this particular declaration is not, however, typical. At first the War led to a relaxation of the campaign against the churches.

Since yesterday our German people has been at war, fighting for the land of its fathers, for the return of German blood to German blood. The German Evangelical Church has always stood in loyal solidarity with the destiny of the German people. To the weapons of steel it has added invincible powers coming from the Word of God: the power of prayer, which strengthens us for good days and ill, and the assurance of the faith that our people, that every single person within it, is in the hands of God. So at this hour too we join with our nation in intercession for the Führer and the Reich, for all the Armed Forces, and for everyone on the home front who is doing his duty for the Fatherland. God grant that we may be found loyal and vouchsafe to us a just peace!

57 An Easy Death for the Incurably Ill

The amazing courage of two men, Pastors Paul Braune and Friedrich von Bodelschwingh, both leading figures in the caritative work of the Protestant Home Mission, who broke through an apparently impregnable cordon of silence and threats by confronting one Ministry after another with the horrific details of the so-called Euthanasia programme, led to the only substantial achievement of the churches during the War: the ending of the systematic extermination of the chronically ill. Braune was arrested by the RHSA in August 1940 but the subsequent publicity given his cause by Bishops Wurm and Galen ensured its success. Hitler's secret authorisation of 1 September 1939 is followed by extracts from Braune's memorandum of July 1940 and a specimen letter to the relatives of the deceased.

(a)

Reichsleiter Bouhler and Dr. Brandt are made responsible for enlarging the competencies of certain doctors — to be named specifically — to enable them to administer an easy death to those who, by human judgement, are incurably ill, after conducting the most careful investigation into their condition.

(b)

In the course of the last few months it has been noticed in various areas of the Reich that a very considerable number of the inmates of the sanatoria and nursing homes are being transferred 'on economic planning grounds' from one home to another, sometimes transferred several times, until several weeks later their relatives receive an intimation of their death. The similarity of the methods, the similarity also of the accompanying circumstances, remove any shadow of doubt that this is a very large-scale action, which is doing away with thousands of people who are 'unfit to live'. It is argued that the defence of the Reich requires us to get rid of these useless mouths. The view is also put forward that the improvement of the genetic stock of the German people makes it necessary to eliminate the mentally sick and other hopeless cases as quickly as possible, together with those who are abnormal, anti-social, or who cannot cope with ordinary community life. It is estimated that about a hundred thousand or more people will be involved. In an article by Professor Kranz in the April edition of the *NS-Volksdienst* the number of those whom it will probably be desirable to eliminate is put as high as a million. It is probable, then, that thousands of fellow-Germans are already being disposed of or are facing imminent death. No legal basis for this action exists. It is imperative that these measures be halted as quickly as possible, as the moral foundations of the nation as a whole are being gravely compromised. The inviolability of human life is one of the basic pillars of every state order. If killing is to be ordered valid laws must be the basis for such measures. It is intolerable that sick men should be being done away with day after day, for reasons of pure expediency, without any careful medical examination, without any legal protection, and without paying any attention to the wishes of their relatives or lawful representatives.

The following facts have been consistently observed:

First, in October 1939 a circular letter from the Reich Minister of the Interior arrived at many sanatoria and nursing homes, and at a number of private institutions which take in patients who are feeble-minded, epileptic, etc. . . . It stated that in view of the necessity for economic planning relating to the sanatoria

85

and nursing homes the enclosed questionnaires should be filled in . . .

. . . As the result of a direct question to the relevant official in the Ministry of the Interior the information was given that the inquiry was purely for statistical purposes. Hence none of the institutions known to me had any hesitations about meeting this request and naming a large number of inmates who apparently came within the terms of the instructions they were given. According to these instructions all patients were to be noted who

1. suffer from the following illnesses and cannot be employed in the institution's work-shops or only at mechanical work (un-ravelling, etc.):
   schizophrenia
   epilepsy (if exogenous, mention war injury or other causes)
   senile illnesses
   incurable paralysis and other syphilitic diseases
   feeble-mindedness of any kind
   encephalitis
   Huntington or other chronic neurological conditions
   or
2. have been in institutions continuously for at least five years
   or
3. are detained as criminally insane
   or
4. are not German citizens or are not of German or related blood, giving race and nationality.

. . . .

On 20 January 1940 the same institutions suddenly received a communication from the Commissar for the Defence of the Reich, a copy of which I enclose. . . . According to this the sick persons were to be transferred in large convoys. It was not desired that relatives should be informed. The whole manner of the communication gave rise to renewed concern as there was no plausible reason why the patients should be transferred.

As far as is known the first comprehensive implementation of these measures has been in the regions:

Pomerania, Brandenburg-Berlin, Saxony, Württemberg, Hamburg

and since June they have been initiated also in most other areas of the Reich.

In the second half of April all the institutions then received very similar communications. . . . These set definite dates for the transfer of the inmates. An enclosed transport list gave the names of the patients who were to be transferred. It now transpired that these names were taken from the lists which had been requested in October and November 1939, allegedly only for statistical purposes.

Then in March 1940 came the news, from Württemberg first of all, that of a transport of 13 epileptics who had been taken from the Pfingstweide to the Grafeneck institution 4 patients had died after only about three weeks. The deaths were normally communicated to the relatives 8-14 days after the patient had died with an almost identical wording in each case. The patients had died suddenly of influenza, pleurisy, cerebral apoplexy, etc. Because of police regulations about infection the corpses had been burnt at once and the clothes incinerated as well. The urns could be collected if desired . . .

To make some estimate of the number of people who have died in Grafeneck I would draw attention to the fact that the urn of Herr Heiner, who died on 10 April 1940, bears the number A 498, while the urn of a certain Max Dreisow, who died at Grafeneck on 12 May 1940, bears the number A 1092, and the urn of Else Lenne, who also died at Grafeneck, on 28 June 1940 . . . already has the number A 3111. Since the whole institution usually has only 100 beds, this can only refer to the number of successive deaths. According to this, in the 33 days from 10 April 1940 to 12 May 1940, 594 people died. This would mean that in an institution with only 100 beds 18 people died each day. In the period from 12 May to 28 June 1940 — 47 days in all — altogether 2019 people died, which means an average of 43 deaths per day in an institution with about 100 beds . . .

. . . .

Visits to institutions in Saxony have made it absolutely clear that mortality has been increased by the withholding of food. The worth of the food given has been reduced to a daily sum of 22-24 Reichpfennige, as I am informed by a reliable source. Since it is quite impossible for the sick people to exist on this they are forcibly given medicine (Paraldehyde) which reduces them to an apathetic state. Verbal and written reports give a frightful account of how the patients cry out again and again, "Hungry, hungry". Employees and nurses who can stand this no longer have occasionally used their private means to still this hunger somewhat but there is no doubt about the end-result. These measures have brought hundreds to a speedy death over the last few months. We are dealing, moreover, not only with patients whose minds are completely numb and apathetic but on the contrary with patients who observe pretty accurately what is going on and see how often burials take place each day. One report pictures the fear of death of one patient who knew only too well what fate was being prepared for himself and his fellow-sufferers.

87

. . . .

. . . In another case the parents of a child did everything possible to track it down until eventually they found it in Brandenburg-Görden. At their second visit they found that the child was already filthy and wretched. They requested that it be returned to one of the Samaritan homes, but were told that there could be no question of this. They were also forbidden to bring the child anything to cheer it up or make its life easier; that, they were told, was quite impossible at present. It seems that frequently patients ripe for death were transferred gradually to the erstwhile penitentiary in Brandenburg where they met their fate in the so-called 'nursing unit'.

. . . .

. . . It was of course natural that these facts should gradually become known among the population, since the relatives of the patients in the sanatoria and nursing homes meet one another on their way to visit the patients and compare notes. This has the effect of shattering confidence in such institutions and especially confidence in doctors and in the authorities. If, however, confidence in the doctor is lost, there is a very real danger that all measures taken by the health service will be regarded with complete suspicion . . .

. . . .

This raises, too, another serious question. How far is the destruction of so-called worthless life going to go? The most recent decree of the same authorities refers to all children born with grave illnesses or deformities, who are to be gathered together and put into special institutions. What awful fears that must give rise to. Will those with tuberculosis be spared? Those in protective custody seem already to be subject to the euthanasia programme. Will it also include other abnormal and anti-social persons? Where is the limit? Who is abnormal, anti-social, or chronically ill? Who is unfit for society? What will happen to the soldiers who succumb to incurable illnesses in fighting for the Fatherland? Such questions are already being discussed in their circles.

. . . .

May those who bear responsibility see to it that these disastrous measures are suspended, and that the whole question is first examined from the legal, medical, ethical, and political point of view before the fate of thousands and tens of thousands has been sealed. *Videant consules, ne quid detrimenti res publica capiat!*

(c)

Frau Marie H —
Berlin —

Dear Frau H,
    We regret deeply that we must inform you that your husband
George H —, who had to be transferred to this institution on
10 September 1940 in accordance with policy decisions taken by
the Commissar for Reich Defence, died here suddenly and un-
expectedly of a heart attack on 23 September 1940.
    In view of his grave mental illness life was a torment for the
deceased. So you must regard his death as a release.
    Since there is at the moment a danger of contagious disease
in this institution the police authorities ordered the immediate
cremation of the corpse.
    Would you please inform us to which cemetery we should ask
the police authorities to transfer the urn containing the mortal
remains of the deceased . . .
    Any enquiries should be addressed to us in writing. Because
of the danger of infection the police have forbidden visits at
present.
    Should we fail to hear from you within 14 days we will have
the urn buried elsewhere free of charge.
    Two death certificates, which you should keep carefully in case
they are required for official purposes, are enclosed.

Heil Hitler!

58 Party and Church during the War, 1940

    Freidrich Schmidt, a member of Rosenberg's staff, and
author of the best-seller, *Das Reich als Aufgabe (The Reich —
Our Task)* speaks for the Party radicals in this assessment of
Christianity and the churches. His own Nordic ideals, on
the other hand, were probably regarded with equal contempt by the sophisticated cynics of the Gestapo, for
example.

1. What about Paragraph 24? Since the two confessions themselves say that Christianity contradicts Germanic attitudes

this point in the Party Programme can be taken as no longer valid as far as the Party is concerned . . .
2. What about the church? Through its bishops the church is now trying to provoke the state. The Party is silent, since the Führer has given a strong directive that nothing should be undertaken against the church at the moment. They can speak and write freely. We are not going to make any martyrs. After the War there will come the reckoning. For we are dealing here with an Either-Or. Christianity is a doctrine from the Near East; it is Jewish through and through. There can be no reconciliation here, such as the German Christians . . . are still trying to propagate.

59 The Exigencies of War, 1940

The actual and alleged needs of the war effort provided a welcome pretext for the confiscation of church buildings, the hindering of meetings, the prohibition of bell-ringing and countless other major and minor measures against the churches. The following directives both date from the end of 1940, the first coming from the Ministry of Labour, the second from the Würzburg office of the Gestapo.

(a)

The shortage of working personnel for Reich defence purposes makes it necessary to exploit every possibility of finding more working personnel. Moreover there is a shortage of new recruits into the professions since years with low birth-rates are now reaching working-age. These circumstances make it imperative that, in the interests of productivity, all able-bodied Germans should be prohibited from entering monasteries or monastic orders.

(b)

According to a decree of the Reich Security Service the staff of the deputy of the Führer and the Reich Minister of Labour agree that Protestant theology candidates, probationary ministers, assistant ministers, etc. who have either been trained at one of the illegal seminaries set up as alternatives to the divinity faculties by the Confessing Front, or who have been illegally ordained, should be classified as unemployed and transferred to a useful occupation, since they have stirred up trouble and exercised a demoralising influence on the population.

60 The Erosion of the Powers of the Ministry for Church Affairs, 2 August 1941

The chaos of competing jurisdictions, always fostered by Hitler, was heightened, as far as Church affairs were concerned, by the progressive elbowing out of Kerrl's ministry—with its dream of a State Church solution—by the anticlerical, anti-Christian radicalism of the SS. This letter sent on 2 August 1941 by Kerrl to Lammers, the State Secretary in the Reich Chancellery, illustrates how his ministry had lost any real power.

As you know, I have clarified my position on the question of the confiscation of monasteries and the closure of monastic establishments in my communication of 11.6.1941-II 2791/41 to the Reich Führer of the SS and Chief of the German Police. Unfortunately I have as yet neither received a reply to this communication on the level of principle, nor am I being informed in individual cases as to what is happening. However I cannot imagine that the manner in which the monasteries are being eliminated while we are engaged in war corresponds with the wishes of the Führer. In 1937 when I requested the Führer to order that the court-cases against countless clergymen, which had been suspended on his instructions, should be taken up again and allowed to take their course, the Führer replied that if this were done he would have to take certain actions regarding the monastic establishments as a result of the court judgements; the time for this, however, was not yet ripe and the court-cases would, accordingly, have to remain in abeyance. Hence I cannot imagine that the Führer considers the present moment to be a particularly appropriate one. As I have already argued in my communication of 11 June 1941, considerations both of internal politics and of foreign policy militate against the elimination of the monasteries during the present war period. However I would not like to miss this opportunity to inform you of my grave concern about the continually mounting number of measures which are being taken against church establishments on the instruction of the state police and of the Party at a time when anything that unnecessarily disturbs the population should be avoided. I have no authority to hinder these measures, although the population puts all the blame for them on me. Hence I feel obliged to inform you of my explicit disapproval of these measures, lest I be made responsible for them to the Führer.

61 The Moratorium on Religious Controversy, 1941

These two confidential directives from 1941, one from Goebbels, the other from Ley, show how the War enabled the Party to clamp down still further on the airing of any theological or ecclesiastical matters deemed controversial, while reserving its own freedom to work for the final reckoning after the War.

(a) Ley, June 1941

. . . The wish of the Führer to postpone the discussion of denominational questions for the duration of the War and to prevent them becoming a matter of controversy should not be taken to mean that any restrictions have been imposed on the Party itself taking a clear stand.

. . . .

(b) Goebbels, 24 August 1941

. . . The War requires an absolute concentration of all the material, mental, and spiritual energies of the nation on victory. Questions which do not relate to this directly, whose solution is not imperative if victory is to be won, have, therefore, no place in public discussion. In particular, the public discussion of questions or problems which will only cause unnecessary offence and spark off harmful controversy is prohibited. . . . To the themes which may not be discussed at the moment, belongs the religious or confessional question.

The Führer has made me responsible for seeing that these and similar themes completely disappear from public discussion. Insofar as they relate to questions which will have to be solved within the framework of the NS programme, the most appropriate solution will be adapted after the War . . .

62 Anonymous Protestant Assessment of the Church Situation 1941-2

This sombre report appears to have been circulated at the tenth Confessing Synod of the Old Prussian Church, meeting secretly at Hamburg in November 1941. The references to the complete absence of any provisions for church life in the Warthegau (carved out of the western part of the occupied Polish territories) indicate the growing awareness in the churches that this might well be the model for the whole Reich in the future.

. . . The Weimar State was no friend of the church. It still was the case, however, that wherever new communities were established, as a matter of course plots of land and building material were set aside for church and manse. The church feasts and the times of church services were respected. Press and radio reckoned with the Christian feelings of the nation, the school affirmed religious instruction in principle, young people could meet together in Christian groupings . . .

How does the situation appear in the winter of 1941/2? Millions of children grow up in Germany without any religious instruction. They do not go to church and they learn nothing about the message of Christ. "Auntie", a seven-year old girl who had been sent to the country asked her new foster mother who had prayed with her on the previous evening, "are you going to make magic with your God again today?" The child had no idea what prayer is. God was an unfamiliar concept to her.

But although there are instances enough of this sort of thing they are apparent only to the person who looks hard and long. The superficial observer may feel that everything is as it was. He would, however, be struck by the total silence about the church in public. Where does one still see posters advertising church meetings? The newspapers are silent. On the whole they do not even print the intimations of church services any more. It is forbidden in Pomerania. The radio, too, is silent. There is nothing Christian in the periodicals. At no exhibition is a Christian work of art to be seen. Scenes of a Christian nature are deleted from plays for the stage. The book-shops display no Christian books, quite apart from the fact that since the Spring of 1941 no Christian literature of any kind is being printed, permission for the use of paper for this purpose being withheld. When those awarded the Ritterkreuz are announced the profession of the father is not disclosed if he is a pastor.

That the church has anything to say about the questions which concern the German people is not even remotely considered. In deep secrecy it is whispered from mouth to mouth throughout Germany that Count Galen, the bishop, has delivered stinging sermons. They are secretly circulated and very widely read. Those in the know also realise that Pastor von Bodelschwingh and the provincial bishop Wurm have spoken out against the killing of the mentally sick, and that pastors sit in concentration camps because they dared to say something against the treatment of the Jews from their understanding of Scripture. Church and Christianity have disappeared from public life.

The old rights of the church vis-a-vis the state have still remained in four points:

1. Many schools still have one or two hours of religious instruction each week. Since there are still a good number of devoted Christians among the older teachers, here and there it is still given in the spirit of the church. In other places, however, this instruction is simply used to combat Christianity. In Saxony the teachers, who had resumed religious instruction after having dropped the subject, were told to include as much Old Testament material as possible, dealing with it in such a way as to innoculate the children against the Jewish-Christian religion.

2. There is still provision in the Army for pastoral care. The restrictions, hindrances, and deconfessionalisation with which it has to contend makes it obvious that it will not outlive this war.

3. The same is true of the theological faculties in the old universities of the Reich.

4. The Ministry for Church Affairs still exists, together with the Finance Departments assigned to the church authorities. . . . Everywhere, however, these are only remnants, well on their way to complete elimination.

The state excludes the church from everything which it considers as belonging to the political sphere. At the same time the church is expected to shrivel up into nothing. As a first step its financial resources are being withdrawn. In the new regions of the Reich no state subsidies at all will be paid. . . . In the old Reich areas they are being reduced year by year. . . . In the Warthegau even collections during the church services are forbidden. Then there are the abrupt confiscations of vast church properties. . . . The fate of the Catholic Church is similar.

After the courageous stand of the Bishop of Münster the Führer issued a 'Stop decree' which could be administered at the discretion of the state secret police. At the disbanding of the courses for mothers in Saxony, for example, it was explained that the church was composed only of the pastor and the consistory; the laity and the organisations were not included. In the Warthegau the churches have just had all their burial grounds taken from them. In the new areas of the Reich church activities on the part of independent organisations no longer exist at all.

. . . .

Since the Spring of 1941 the cases of Party speakers bluntly advocating the liquidation of Christianity have been multiplying. In the Old March (Brandenburg): Magdeburg Cathedral will remain as a cultural monument, "but your Halleluja-halls here, they'll all have to come down, or we'll turn them into pigsties." . . .

. . . .

There is still noticeable resistance. Resistance in the Catholic Church seems to be becoming determined and firm now after a long period of evasion and compromise. The political authorities had avoided repeating the mistakes of the *Kulturkampf* in dealing with her and tried to ruin her moral standing with the immorality trials. Now films are being produced which are supposed to demonstrate that only the combination of brute force with monastic hypocrisy was able to force Christianity upon the noble Germans . . .

The immorality trials compelled the Catholic Church to use extreme reserve in defending itself. Apart from some isolated pointed remarks by Cardinal Faulhaber there was a strange reticence. The expulsion of the bishop of Rottenburg, for example, caused far less uproar than the house-arrest of the Evangelical provincial bishops Wurm and Meiser at an earlier stage. Even the confiscation of many monasteries and the abolition of religious instruction did not provoke any perceptible reaction.

Not until after the summer of 1941 did the situation alter. There is now a determination to speak frankly and act courageously. It is true that the anticipated papal encyclical has not yet materialised, probably in order to avoid the Pope appearing as the ally of Stalin. But the action taken by Bishop Galen in

Münster was no individual sally; it is backed by the decisions of this year's bishops' conference at Fulda. The Bishop of Trier, Bornewasser, has also held sermons in the cathedral on the situation in regard to the education of young people and on the destruction of worthless life. In Cologne Catholic mothers compelled the Lord Provost to restore already confiscated nursery schools. In many places the decree of the Ministry of the Interior forbidding the customary practice in regard to baptisms and pastoral visits in all hospitals, even the confessional ones, is at the moment either no longer being observed or has yet to be observed because of the protests raised by Catholic and Evangelical mothers. On the Evangelical side the sympathies for the Führer and for National Socialism have always been stronger and even today this is still the case on the whole. It was this after all which brought about the German Christian take-over of the church authorities. Today this trust in the Führer contends desperately with a realisation of the truth. Even in the Confessing Church organisations in the Wuppertal a rumour was circulating recently that Hitler had experienced a conversion, that he now confesses the Christian faith and like Bismarck before him reads the daily lectionary of the Moravian Brethren . . .

63 The Ambivalent Attitude of the Churches During the War, 7 November 1941

This protest from Dr. Kottmann, Vicar General of the diocese of Rottenburg, was prompted by the confiscation of church buildings, and was sent to the Ministry of Internal Affairs on 7 November 1941. The arguments used, of course, are calculated to appeal to the NS authorities; they probably also reflect a fair degree of personal conviction.

. . . .

The fact that so many believing soldiers are among the lists of the fallen justifies the conclusion that it is above all those soldiers with true Christian beliefs who have helped to win the great victories. Already in the First World War it was the Catholic theologians who, next to the officers of the professional Army, could boast the highest percentage of casualties. The soldierly virtues and those of faith are mutually dependent as the example of Hindenburg shows.

These believing dead heroes sought to fight against unbelieving Bolshevism. But they certainly did not fight or give their life in order to have that which they hold holy fought against in the homeland. Let an end be put at long last to the fight against all that is Christian in the homeland and restore to us the good old laws . . .

64 War Atrocities, 28 January 1943

This memorandum addressed to Dr. Dill, a senior official in the Ministry of the Interior in Stuttgart, is one of a whole series of protests sent by Bishop Wurm to Hitler, Goebbels, and others, as he realised the anti-Christian course which, in his view, the War was now taking. Such protests were, of course, private, but none the less courageous for that. If the arch-patriotism of men like Wurm and Galen had blinded them previously to the nature of National Socialism they now made their abhorrence quite clear.

. . . .

Apart from these church concerns in the narrower sense of the word I must mention a very explosive and difficult issue which unfortunately cannot be side-stepped. The manner in which the war is being conducted against other races and peoples is causing widespread depression, and not only within the Christian confessions. One learns from holiday-makers to what extent the systematic murder of Jews and Poles is taking place in the occupied territories. Even those of us who, at a time when almost the whole Press was philo-semitic, regarded the predominance of Judaism in the various spheres of public live as a grave defect, cannot agree that one people is justified in liquidating another by measures which embrace every single individual irrespective of his personal guilt or innocence. It is contrary to the clear command of God to bring about the death of people who have been convicted of no crime simply because they belong to another race or because their health is not good. It is contrary also to the concepts of justice and humanity without which no cultured people can exist. There can be no blessing on such actions. It is

97

worth considering that since these methods began to be used the successes which were the lot of German arms at the beginning of the war have no longer been coming their way. Many of our fellow-countrymen not only regard such goings-on as distressing but as involving us in a guilt for which there may be a bitter revenge. They would sigh with relief if a courageous and generous decision of the state leadership were to do away with everything which stains German honour. The Evangelical Church has kept silence about this in public to avoid exposing the shame of the German people to foreign eyes. If, however, at this time the nation is being asked to make further great sacrifices, it should be granted relief from this weight on its conscience.

. . . .

65 The Religious Press during the War, 3 January 1943

This letter of Archbishop Bertram to the Minister of Church Affairs on 3 January 1943 protests against the closing down of many church publishers.

. . . .

The watch-word on every lip in the present situation: *Fight against Bolshevism* in order to safeguard German and European culture, would meet with widespread incomprehension both within Germany and in other European countries . . . [if religious publishing firms were closed down]. At all times, but particularly now, amidst all the hardships of war, the Christian faith and the Christian Church are sources of quite exceptional strength and comfort to the faithful. The religious literature of the church, therefore, is an indispensable factor in promoting a spirit of the utmost self-sacrifice and the most resolute endurance throughout the nation.

66 The Final Solution, 17 October 1943

At the twelfth Confessing Synod of the Old Prussian Union held in Breslau in October 1943 the moral problems raised by the War were dealt with in a lengthy interpretation of the Fifth Commandment. This condemned any 'liquidation' of people on grounds of race and chronic ill-health. All human life was declared sacred, "including the life of the people of Israel." The statement prepared by the Synod for reading from the pulpit is as close as any of the Christian churches came to a public condemnation of the Final Solution.

. . . Woe unto us and our nation, when the life which God has given is held in contempt and man, made in the image of God, is regarded in purely utilitarian terms; when the killing of men is justified on the grounds that they are unfit to live or that they belong to another race; when hate and callousness become widespread. For God says: "Thou shalt not kill."
. . . .
Let us confess with shame: We Christians share the guilt for the contempt and perversion of the holy Commandments. We have often kept our silence; we have pled too seldom, too timidly, or not at all, for the absolute validity of God's holy Commandments. . .

67 Statistics on the Membership and Finances of the Churches, 3 July 1944

On the request of the Ministry for Popular Enlightenment and Propaganda Kerrl sent Goebbels these statistics on 3 July 1944, with the rather anxious request that caution be used in their exploitation for propaganda purposes. It is worth noting how little success the National Socialists had in weaning people away from their adherence to Christian beliefs. Only 3.5% acknowledged themselves as *Gottgläubige* (Neo-Paganism).

. . . .
A *Religious Allegiance*
According to the results of the national census of 17 May 1939 the Greater German Reich contained at that time (not including the protectorates of Bohemia and Moravia) a resident population of   79,375,381
of which there belonged to a church, religious society, or a religious/ideological community   75,393,799

These are sub-divided as follows:
Members of the Protestant Provincial Churches or Free
Churches   42,636,150 = 54%
Members of the Roman Catholic Church including those follow-
ing the rites of the Uniate churches   31,944,000 = 40%
Believers in God *(Gottgläubige)*   2,745,893 = 3.5%
Unbelievers   1,208,005 = 1.5%
. . . .

C *Assets of the Churches . . . in the Old Reich in 1937*
1. Protestant Churches

	Area	Value (RM)
(a) Agricultural and forest land	390,708.87 hectars	328,388,805
(b) Dwellings of clergy and church officials (including 15,941 manses)		195,421,656
(c) Other Property . . .		108,960,196
Total:		632,770,657

2. Roman Catholic Church

	Area	Value (RM)
(a) Agricultural and forest land	206,682.02 hectars	184,465,295
(b) Dwellings of clergy and church officials		134,921,167
(c) Other property . . .		128,919,672
Total:		448,306,134

. . . .

4. Property of the Protestant foundations and
   institutions (Home Mission etc.)   52,230,710
5. Property of the Catholic Orders and
   Congregations . . .   143,239,081

Not included under 1-3 are properties exempt from land-tax
(churches, chapels, church administrative buildings, seminars
for preachers and priests, congregational halls in so far as they
are used for the purpose of worship and religious instruction. . .).
The art treasures, libraries, etc. contained in the churches are
also not listed. Their value could not in any case be estimated.
. . . .

D *Subsidies from the Reich and the Provinces*
Have been paid to the churches since 1933 as follows: (in the
territories of the Old Reich as they were on 1 January 1938,
Saarland from 1936)

in the financial year 1933	113,890,000 RM
1934	113,130,000
1935	105,100,000
1936	95,836,117
1937	88,165,547
1938	86,065,299

100

1939	72,366,843
1940	69,403,973
1941	68,402,033
1942	72,104,582
1943	71,574,782

Total: 956,066,226 RM

. . . .

B The Income Derived by the churches from the church-tax amounted in the territories of the Old Reich to:

1938
Protestant Provincial Churches	221,500,000 RM
Catholic Dioceses	94,700,000

. . . .

1939
Protestant Provincial Churches	227,900,000 RM
Catholic Dioceses	105,100,000

. . . .

1940
Protestant Provincial Churches	238,893,000 RM
Catholic Dioceses	116,049,000

68 Trial of Jehovah's Witnesses, 18 November 1944

Naturally the War provoked still fiercer persecution of the pacifistic Jehovah's Witnesses. The extract is taken from the case for the prosecution of fourteen Jehovah's Witnesses before the Berlin Supreme Court.

. . . The writing, 'Look the Facts in the Face', has the impertinence to launch vicious attacks on the leadership of the National Socialist state. It argues, inter alia, thus:

"Moreover, we have to face the further, undeniable fact, which stands in direct contradiction to the righteous rule of God, that there has of late appeared upon the earth a hideous monster, which — in complete disregard of the inalienable rights of man — is engaged in the rapid seizure of power and dominion over the world, in reducing men to mindless obedience and slavery. People are terrified of the monster and submit to it in craven fear.

. . . .

All nations on earth have to face the same situation. Hence none of them should be prejudiced against another because of preconceptions and partisanship, because of race, nationality, or colour. God has made all nations which dwell upon the earth of one blood, and everyone has the right to the same impartial treatment.

What, then, is this hideous monster? It is the totalitarian government or dictatorship, which makes the state supreme, reduces all men to mindless obedience, rules over them by arbitrary despots and forces everyone to render them unconditional obedience. This monster is, therefore, a deceitful aping of God's righteous rule . . ."

Sources

1. *Kirchliches Jahrbuch für die evangelische Kirche in Deutschland 1933-44*, pp. 2-3.
2. *Zwischen den Zeiten*, 8 (1930), pp. 1ff.
3. *Kirchliches Jahrbuch*, pp. 4-6. (KJ)
4. Hans Müller, *Katholische Kirche und Nationalsozialismus*, pp. 62-63.
5. KJ, pp. 8-12.
6. *Ibid.*, p. 13.
7. Müller, *op.cit.*, pp. 88-89.
8. *Ibid.*, pp. 98-99.
9. KJ, p. 14.
10. A. Boyens, *Kirchenkampf und Ökumene 1933-39*, pp. 299-308.
11. H. Hermelink, *Kirche im Kampf*—Dokumente des Widerstands und des Aufbaus in der Evangelischen Kirche Deutschlands von 1933 bis 1945, p. 32.
12. *Ibid.*, p. 35.
13. Müller, *op.cit.*, pp. 118-131.
14. Hermelink, *op.cit.*, pp. 37-38.
15. Müller, *op.cit.*, pp. 178-179.
16. KJ, pp. 17-20.
17. Müller, *op.cit.*, p. 179.
18. KJ, p. 21.
19. *Ibid.*, pp. 21-22.
20. *Ibid.*, pp. 22-23.
21. Werner Weber, *Die deutschen Konkordate und Kirchenverträge der Gegenwart*, pp. 15-32.
22. Müller, *op.cit.*, pp. 190-196.
23. W. Niemöller, *Texte zur Geschichte des Pfarrernotbundes*, pp. 22-23, 26.
24. F. Zipfel, *Kirchenkampf in Deutschland 1933-45*, p. 270.
25. *Junge Kirche*, I (1933), p. 363.
26. Manfred Priepke, *Die Evangelische Jugend im Dritten Reich 1933-36*, p. 186.

27. *Junge Kirche*, 2 (1934), p. 72.
28. Hermelink, *op.cit.*, pp. 66-67.
29. *Ibid.*, pp. 83-84.
30. *Arbeiten zur Geschichte des Kirchenkampfes* (AgK) 6, 196-203.
31. Zipfel, *op.cit.*, pp. 271-272.
32. *Ibid.*, p. 294.
33. AgK 3, pp. 37-38.
34. Zipfel, *op.cit.*, pp. 326-327, 332.
35. Hauer, *Deutsche Gottschau*, pp. 1-3, 42, 75.
36. Hermelink, *op.cit.*, pp. 287-288.
37. AgK 13, 33-37.
38. Karl Altmeyer, *Katholische Presse unter NS-Diktatur*, p. 141.
39. AgK 13, 695-719.
40. Hubert Mohr, *Katholische Orden und Deutscher Imperialismus*, pp. 284-285.
41. AgK 14, 1154-1156.
42. KJ, p. 162.
43. AgK 14, 1358-1362.
44. Arthur Utz, *La Doctrine Sociale de l'Église à traveits les Siècles*, I, 286-324.
45. KJ, pp. 197-201.
46. Zipfel, *op.cit.*, p. 423.
47. KJ, pp. 224-225.
48. Mohr, *op.cit.*, p. 294.
49. Zipfel, *op.cit.*, pp. 450-451.
50. Hermelink, *op.cit.*, pp. 453-454.
51. KJ, pp. 263-265.
52. Zipfel, p. 458.
53. *Ibid.*, pp. 486-489.
54. KJ, p. 296.
55. *Ibid.*, pp. 363-364; 391.
56. *Ibid.*, p. 473.
57. Hans Christoph von Hase, *Evangelische Dokumente zur Ermordung der unheilbar Kranken unter der NS Herrschaft 1939-1945*, pp. 8, 14-22; Zipfel, *op.cit.*, pp. 503-540.
58. Gerhard Schäfer, *Landesbischof D. Wurm und der NS Staat 1940-45*, p. 22.
59. Zipfel, *op.cit.*, pp. 505-507.
60. Mohr, *op.cit.*, p. 328.
61. Zipfel, *op.cit.*, p. 509; KJ, pp. 467-468.
62. *Ibid.*, pp. 382-386.
63. Mohr, *op.cit.*, p. 330.
64. Hermelink, *op.cit.*, pp. 562-565.
65. Mohr, *op.cit.*, p. 157.
66. KJ, pp. 402-404.
67. Mohr, *op.cit.*, pp. 336-339.
68. Zipfel, *op.cit.*, pp. 527-533.